Visual Perversity

Visual Perversity

A Re-articulation of Maternal Instinct

Alina M. Luna

LEXINGTON BOOKS
Lanham • Boulder • New York • Toronto • Oxford

LEXINGTON BOOKS

Published in the United States of America
by Lexington Books
An imprint of The Rowman & Littlefield Publishing Group, Inc.
4501 Forbes Boulevard, Suite 200, Lanham, Maryland 20706

PO Box 317
Oxford
OX2 9RU, UK

British Library Cataloguing in Publication Information Available

Library of Congress Cataloging-in-Publication Data

Luna, Alina M., 1970–
Visual perversity : a re-articulation of maternal instinct / Alina M. Luna.
p. cm.
Includes bibliographical references and index.
ISBN 0-7391-0870-0 (cloth : alk. paper)
1. Motherhood in literature. 2. Motherhood in motion pictures. 3. Love, Maternal, in literature. 4. Mother and child in literature. I. Title.
PN56.5.M67L86 2004
809′.933552—dc22

2004010689

Printed in the United States of America

™ The paper used in this publication meets the minimum requirements of American National Standard for Information Sciences—Permanence of Paper for Printed Library Materials, ANSI/NISO Z39.48–1992.

For Anthony—because we have always been

Contents

Acknowledgments ix

Introduction
Seeing Not to See: The Idiomatic Eye 1

1 (Re)membering to Mother in Euripides' *Bacchae* 13

2 A Breast to Dream of, Not to Tell: Re-birth in "Christabel" 31

3 To Spare a Fly and Harm a Son: Hitchcock's Norma Bates 53

4 Breaking the Bond: Eugenie's Triumph in the Bedroom 77

Conclusion
Eyeing the Margins 101

Selected Bibliography 103

Index 107

About the Author 109

Acknowledgments

I would like to thank Charlie Shepherdson, Tom Cohen, and Pierre Joris for reading my work and offering comments and encouragement. I have also had wonderfully helpful editors at Lexington, particularly in Robert Carley who graciously and patiently saw me and this book through, as well as Kim Smith, Brian Richards, Rebekka Brooks, and Amy Ford. I am grateful to those who granted permission to reprint excerpts from songs and articles: Jennifer Chartier and Hal Leonard Corporation, Hope Chirino and Warner Bros. Publications, Matt Smith and International Music Publications Ltd., and Courtroom Television Network LLC. The epigraph to *Visual Perversity* is reproduced by permission of the Estate of Angela Carter c/o Rogers, Coleridge & White Ltd., 20 Powis Mews, London W11 1JN. Copyright © 1978 Angela Carter. Use of the cover photograph was arranged by Coi Drummond-Gehrig and Trina Purcell on behalf of the Denver Public Library's Western History Collection.

I must acknowledge Tom Cook for having taught all the literary periods I came to love as an undergraduate and Gladys Craig for her strength and dry humor; my friends and colleagues: Jenn Richardson, Pedro Monteiro, Pete Monaco, and Jeff Berman for their confidence and enthusiasm; Kerry and Lenny Valure for their artistic eyes; my students who kept me sharp; and my family.

This text would not exist without the support of two people. My debt to Helen Elam is one I am happy to owe. For her patience, guidance, and dedication to my work, she has been an incomparable adviser—but her friendship and affection have endeared her to me. She has nurtured my intellect and proven that some of the best mothers are not mothers at all.

And to Anthony Miccoli, a loving husband and gifted professor who suffered with me in my writing and my often theatrical displays of despair just so he could lighten my mood. You have understood my work (sometimes painfully so) and had such faith and pride in me. In many ways you are already more than I will ever deserve.

This theory of maternal superiority is one of the most damaging of all consolatory fictions and women themselves cannot leave it alone, although it springs from the timeless, placeless, fantasy island of archetypes where all the embodiments of biological supremacy live.

—*Angela Carter,* The Sadeian Woman

Introduction

Seeing Not to See: The Idiomatic Eye

Of what are the eyes capable—these organs of sight which, although varying in color from person to person, are fairly indistinguishable.[1] They are not capable of many physical actions, but the few motions of which they are cannot escape scrutiny and interpretation. Rapidly looking from side to side signifies an untrustworthy or "shifty-eyed" person. One whose eyes remain fixed to a specific spot is either staring and, therefore, rude or is regarded as having a vacant look which translates into stupidity. A person must be on constant guard that his eyes do not move too much or too little. Even one whose eyes may be considered slightly "abnormal" cannot escape some sort of derogatory ocular characterization. "Lazy-eyed" refers to someone with an eye unable to establish central vision/perception, yet has normal peripheral vision. The term "wall-eyed" is for someone whose one eye tends to linger in one spot, often toward the side or wall, despite the other eye looking straight ahead. It seems to lack the speed of the "good" eye, capable of only sluggish movement. And of course there is "cross-eyed," a term that not only denotes one whose eyes "focus" on one's nose, but also signifies an occasion for laughter and ridicule (which we would all like to think confines itself to the realm of elementary school). These last two conditions not only discomfort the one afflicted but also those with whom he comes in contact. Because so much value is placed upon "eye contact" (another curious phrase bent on establishing the illusion that some physical interaction has taken place), there is an immediate demand made on the one with whom the "wall/cross-eyed" person is communicating: into which eye should one look? Either way, a feeling of awkwardness is inescapable. If one looks into the "bad" eye, then one is rude. To look at the "good" eye requires some effort since that which is different or out of the ordinary tends to catch one's attention. One's only recourse, then, is to focus on the bridge of the nose, which means that although one is not looking into the other's eyes, his gaze maintains a close proximity to where it would be if he were. In a case such as this, it is difficult to maintain "eye contact" because the other's line of vision appears to fork toward two different paths. Does all of this then mean that he has failed to deal honestly with the other since he only created the illusion that he was looking into the other's eyes when he indeed was not?

I Could Tell by the Look of You

One's first and immediate mode of knowing another is through sight, and one's capacity to judge others based on appearances seems to be a consequence of this. Those who seek to deceive are sometimes characterized as having "lying eyes," and having "seen through them" is often an occasion for self-congratulation. But the ability to tell that these are indeed "lying eyes" is not so much the result of clever detection as it is due to a sort of infringement of one sense upon another. This is an instance in which the eyes overstep, since lying traditionally belongs to the realm of the spoken word. In this case the mouth fails to utter a falsity which is then expressed by the eyes.

The demand "look me in the eyes and say that" implies that the ability to do so is some guarantor of truth. Inasmuch as it may be an effort to achieve honesty, it is also an admission that one's other senses have failed to discriminate between a truth and a falsity, thereby investing vision and the eye with superiority. Here, believing or disbelieving a statement is determined not so much by the earnestness of one's voice as it is by the steadiness of one's gaze, the likes of which attest to the sincerity of one's words.

You've Got the Look

The eye itself is an illusion. Although palpable, it is a fragile object implying weakness, thus, denoting a lack of durability. There are certainly other organs which could withstand more than an eye could. With no more than a thin sheath of skin to protect it from the outer world, its safety can be a tenuous one. Yet despite, or perhaps because of, this very fragility, the power of the eye has obviously been given testimony by a plethora of idiomatic expressions.

Eyes are the window to the soul. Those whom I suspect desire to see the ultimate unseen, the soul, look to the eye as the window into which they may peer to gain knowledge of it. The eye becomes that through which one may glimpse a spiritual plane as well as a physical manifestation of the condition of one's soul, a condition which may be caused by one's ocular actions, as in the case of the "shifty-eyed" person. And what quality of soul would one see in another who was lazy/cross-eyed, or even more frighteningly, one with a vacant stare? If one chooses to believe that the eye can see beyond the physical into the immaterial or essence of someone, then what comfort is available when one peers in only to find nothing? If the window is the eye in its entirety, then the pane of glass must be the pupil which appears to be a perfectly round hole in the eye, a hole that connotes depth. Yet the pupil, despite its appearance, is indeed bounded, has a physical substance, and can be touched (though painfully so). And so this depth into which we search out the soul is an illusion which presents the seeker with a black void.[2] It may be that by equating the vacant stare with someone stupid, one attempts to escape this shattering possibility of nothingness, for synonymous with the word "stupid" are the phrases "empty upstairs" and "nothing in the head."

Perhaps instead the eye is the window through which we glimpse the (biological) essence of all mortal life, an essence which is only apparent in a photograph. At times, a person will be photographed with "red-eye" caused by a camera flash reflecting off of the retina. The color, however, is derived from the blood vessels in the eye. It is by way of the photograph that one sees his own blood, the blood which signifies life, without being wounded or feeling pain. The appearance of "red-eye," however, is undesirable and often "ruins" an otherwise "perfect" picture; it often makes one appear to have "demon eyes." Perhaps this demonic characterization is a true testament to the soul within.

What Big Eyes You Have!

The eye tends to be empowered with destructive forces which leave a residue on the more erotic or amorous expressions. "I only have eyes for you" is a declaration of devotion, but a devotion that is blind to everything else can easily become obsession. "I undressed him with my eyes" speaks to an erotic desire that objectifies and violates the other, a peeling off of one's outer "skin." "I could drown in his eyes," despite its surface sweetness, is actually the willingness to seek one's self-destruction by way of complete immersion in another. It is a desire for death evoked by the very depths of another's eyes.

Although "seeing red" signifies a blinding rage, one may also redirect his/her anger while skirting physical violence. The idiomatic expressions which characterize these angered looks tend to be extreme. "Her eyes shot daggers" and "If looks could kill, he'd be dead" express sentiments more lethal than any punch to the stomach. These are looks that pierce and murder and can elicit a response such as "It hurts the way you look at me." The eye suddenly becomes capable of inflicting pain that reeks of malevolence and seeks the annihilation of the other. If another's figurative destruction will not suffice, there is always recourse to the "evil eye," a curse that seeks its fulfillment not just in the other's psychological or emotional discomfort, but in more palpable terms that jeopardize the physical body. How does one locate the boundary between these instances of ill will and those of eroticism? The distinction may lie in a single word, as in "I wanted to eat him up" and "I wanted to eat him alive." Although both pertain to the act of devouring, the former connotes amorous (delicious) possession while the latter implies a desire for the other to consciously witness ("alive") and suffer through his own demise.

These destructive forces which vision seems to inspire find their articulation in de Sade, who attempts to overlay the psychological affliction of lack upon the body. That which is hidden in the reflection of wholeness is revealed by him in strictly corporeal terms. It is as if the body were punished for its deceit, for a lie it has been perpetuating. By antithetically punishing the body—the ripping away of skin and filling of orifices—he reveals that which was meant to be hidden (muscles, tissue, etc.) and fills that which should remain empty. The infliction of such unnatural conditions upon the body is, at times, exacerbated by instances of coprophilia: the body is compelled to satisfy its physical hunger or another's fetishistic desires through the ingestion of excremental by-products. That which the body needs and wants is found and supplied by another body, suggestive of a cannibalistic quality that denotes each character as existing for the consumption of another. De Sade's predilection for flatulence also indicates an interest in the unseen/intangible which nevertheless is present. The eventual dispersion of it, its fleetingness, signifies its always already non-presence/absence. The coprophilic element betrays a fascination with the body's capacity for excessive fullness which demands expulsion. That a number of de Sade's characters eat excrement bespeaks an inability to let go of that which must necessarily result in a space in the bowels, an empty stomach, a lack within the body. To consume it is to negate its status as "waste," and its disappearance denies its existence—both of which refute the belief that the body can ever be too full or complete.

Mothers Have Eyes in the Backs of Their Heads

My text opens with a chapter on Euripides' *Bacchae*, followed by sections on Samuel Taylor Coleridge's "Christabel," Alfred Hitchcock's *Psycho*, and the Marquis de Sade's *Philosophy in the Bedroom*. Although I am interested in the workings of vision as a whole, my great fascination lies in sight that evokes the desire for another's destruction, when the sought-after objective of knowing another can only be achieved at the expense of the other's physical and/or psychological demise. My work is not a study of the male gaze that supposedly objectifies woman into sheer passivity, stripping her of identity and capitalizing on her "to-be-looked-at-ness" or castrated condition as Laura Mulvey contends.[3] It is, instead, an exploration into the maternal gaze as represented within the Western literary tradition,[4] informed by a desire to re-possess the child even at the cost of the latter's well-being. The all-consuming narcissism demanded and validated by pregnancy does not end with the child's expulsion from the womb. The mother looks upon the child in the same manner as Sartre looks upon the world: as always for her. The Sartrian idea of nothingness at the core of one's being undergoes a strangely physical articulation in the figure of the mother-having-given-birth. The empty womb signifies the literal nothingness occasioned by the child's evacuation, the same nothingness which the maternal feels compelled to deny. The physicality and intimacy of pregnancy serve as the foundation for the abstract notion of the mother-child bond, which the maternal articulates through her desire for the child's visual presence. This, thereby, creates the illusion that the nothingness at the core of her being produced not nothing but its opposite: *thing*. The connotation of object which accompanies "thing," also known as child, allows the maternal to exert its will over the child with self-centeredness and unyielding prejudice. In the end, it is not the male gaze that is most damaging, but the maternal one.

There is often the sense that one cannot escape the gaze of the maternal, especially when one is involved in improper conduct. The ability of mothers to know what their children are doing without being within visible proximity of their activities becomes translated into an odd idiomatic mutation.[5] Although this notion of eyes on the back of one's head can pertain to anyone capable of knowing without having seen, the maternal power as a whole seems to have laid claim to this mysterious ability, as evidenced by the many complaints of both children and adults.

This monopoly of an all-seeing capacity can be a haunting one, particularly for the offspring, because knowledge and surveillance become synonymous with the maternal. Having been delivered from a body, one finds that there is no escape from the place of its conception. The gestation period during which one develops in the womb is a maternally internalized scopic field that may mislead one to believe that this is a temporary state of gazing/surveillance, the end of which is signified by the birth of the infant. This, however, is not the case. Once expelled from the maternal body, a heightened sense of being watched is triggered by conduct that would meet with maternal disapproval. The actions of the offspring are then prone to the influences of the mother by the pre-existing condition of having been the object of the womb's constant gazing, the center of attention. The propriety of an act is not always an issue of right or wrong as much as it can sometimes be whether it would meet with approval or disapproval of the mother. The maternal then becomes a type of moral signifier, the likes of which the child may feel compelled to circumvent or overthrow. The all-seeingness of the eyes in the back of the head, however, makes such an attempt seem almost impossible. The sense of ownership conferred upon the mother by having birthed another, coupled with a confining existence within her gaze, exacerbate what can only be ambivalent feelings on the part of the child. The chapters with which I begin and end (*The Bacchae* and *Philosophy in the Bedroom* respectively) demonstrate extreme reactions informed by that maternal sense of ownership and the child's resulting ambivalence.

In *The Bacchae*, Pentheus is introduced as a king of Thebes with a willingness to hunt down his own mother for worshipping Dionysus. Although this wish temporarily supplants any affection toward her, Pentheus later affirms their filial connection in an attempt to save his own life. Pentheus the man is forced to assert himself as Pentheus the son/child, to regress in the hope of being spared by his mother. To spare a life, however, is also to give it, which carries implications of ownership and possession, of the right to do with it as one pleases. In a sadeian world, Pentheus is the cause of his own undoing by posing himself as a possession, as someone whose fate lies in the hands of (belongs to) another. Although de Sade circumvents the exertion of maternal authority by asserting that one's offspring never consciously asks to be born, and, thus, owes no duty to the mother who has instead inflicted life upon her child, Pentheus asks to be given his life, a mere request, whose only weight relies upon a filial bond toward which Pentheus himself has been ambivalent. As he swore that his mother and other worshipers of Dionysus would be "hunted down / out of the mountains like the animals they are" (ll.228-9),[6] so too does his mother literally see him as an animal, one who cannot be linguistically understood, one whose words cannot be heard. That he himself suffers the very torments he had previously wished upon others is not only a disturbing example of the literalizing power of the word, but also emphasizes an aspect of Dionysus' own power, for he is a god who follows and acts upon the words of others.

Pentheus' attempt to spy on the secret activities of the bacchae results in his discovery and confrontation with his mother, Agave. Aware of the danger to his well-being, he discards his wig, touches her cheek, and says, "No, no, Mother, I am Pentheus, / your own son, the child you bore to Echion! / Pity me, spare me, Mother! I have done a wrong / but do not kill your own son for my offense" (ll.1118-21). Agave's incapacity to recognize her own child is almost unfathomable. How can a mother not know the child whom she has not only given birth to but also raised? Face to face with a distance easily negotiated by an outreached hand, Agave is unable to recognize Pentheus. The touch of his hand upon her cheek is inconsequential as is the sound of his voice—intimacy seems to escape her. His statements mean nothing to her and instead she sees him as a talking beast that must be killed. Agave's alienation is not only from Pentheus but herself as well and indicates a psychic fragmentation. Her lack of recognition abandons Pentheus to what seems to be a necessary death which is initiated by her very own hands. Agave's own internal fragmentation and its severity become reflected in the scattering of Pentheus' limbs and the distances to which they are flung. His dismemberment is wrought by the failure of Agave's vision and as such becomes compensated for by the sheer physicality of the manner in which she attacks him. The attack is then proof of two seemingly disparate ideas: his death is both testimony to Agave's psychic fragmentation that prevents her from recognizing him and perversely proof of the subtext that informs, shapes, and creeps beneath maternal vision—that desire for the physical appropriation of the child, the same desire that erupts and is achieved once maternal vision fails. Maternal vision, therefore, appears to be a channel through which the desire for a child's destruction is channeled/dissipated.

The desecration of Pentheus' body, the ripping away of flesh, and the playing with scraps of his body is a reflection of his status as thing; its further fragmentation leaves him barely identifiable, thus, imposing a degree of difficulty strangely akin to Agave's own and upon those sent to gather his remains. The treatment that attends a thing is often without forethought or reflection, and as such Agave is unable to recall what she has done to her own son. The re-establishment of her memory is made possible by Cadmus and the literal re-formation of, and confrontation with, the thing as son.

The dismemberment of his body seems to imply that the maternal gaze is only capable of recognizing the child not as a whole entity unto himself, but as a fragmented being constantly dependent upon his mother. By bringing his head, Agave makes it possible for the people to identify what remains of an otherwise anonymous body. The re-establishment of his identity then becomes (physically) dependent upon his mother's arrival with his head. Now fragmented, Pentheus' body can only regain some semblance of wholeness once the parts are gathered together once again. As a living and intact being, his mother fails to recognize him as her son and as a young man. Killing him re-establishes and freezes a moment of child-like desperation and dependence, the likes of which had been displaced by his maturation. His need for her to recognize him, articulated by his frantic pleas, is later given visual realization/testimony by this "reliance" upon Agave who must carry his head back into Thebes. Inasmuch as the very horror of a mother bearing her own son's head creates a spectacle for the Thebans, there is another more frightening notion that must, perhaps out of necessity, escape them. In the failure of Agave's gaze to dissipate that destructive wish to possess her child, the act of murdering Pentheus becomes the literalization of maternal desire itself. It is only the sheer horror of the spectacle that safeguards us all from this realization. Her recognition of Pentheus' head not only ensures the correction of her sight, but also the propriety of her punishment.

Pentheus' death at the hands of his own mother is "reversed" in Eugenie's defilement of the mother-child bond in *Philosophy in the Bedroom*, a text in which ambivalent feelings toward the maternal find their most brutal expression. Eugenie who is first introduced as daughter and pupil, both of which connote a degree of subservience, redirects the loathing felt toward the maternal into the means by which she is able to elevate herself to a position of power over her mother. Pentheus, who had no such "success," suffers instead as Eugenie's foil.

Madame de Mistival attempts to retrieve her daughter, Eugenie, from her lessons in libertinage. Unable to regain possession of her child, she interferes by invoking her status as Eugenie's mother, which she believes will re-establish her control over daughter's behavior. Her attempts, however, only provide Eugenie with the opportunity to prove how much she has learned from her tutors. Given that pain is the path to pleasure, it is then possible to read Eugenie's violation of her mother as an act not simply wrought by pure hatred, but also from a desire to please. If Eugenie has learned from Dolmance as much as she claims and seems to have, then it is impossible for her to ignore that great pain leads to even greater pleasure. Her acts of hatred cannot completely mitigate an irrepressible affection. Eugenie's claim, "I'm going to teach you to be a libertine,"[7] is not only a wish to become master over her mother but also a desire to share what she has now become with her mother. It is a desire to induct her mother into a lifestyle that Eugenie feels is superior to the one which the former inhabits, that is, as one no longer defined by her own desires but by her role in society. Eugenie annihilates the status of mother which attends Madame de Mistival for the sake of the latter's re-birth into a life bereft of the maternal, that is, to elevate her to the status of woman before the contamination of motherhood and its attendant self-sanctification takes hold. By bringing her mother to orgasm she initiates an inversion in which mother becomes woman at the hands of her daughter. However, unlike the oblivion from which Eugenie emerges as an eager protégé, Madame de Mistival re-gains consciousness only to refuse the lessons being taught to her by her daughter. The "life's horrors" into which she is re-awakened testify to her inability to elevate herself above the status of victim, a status to which she had been assigned by her abusive husband. Unwilling to acknowledge that she too can gain (sexual) pleasure from the horrors of life, she proves herself unworthy of the lessons being given. Not only does she embrace her status as victim, but she also refuses to relinquish her status as mother, her last words to her daughter being, "You are tearing me to pieces, vile creature! . . . Oh, how I blush that it was I who gave you life!" (364). After Eugenie violates her mother with a phallus and sanctions her rape by a syphilitic, Eugenie seals her mother's vagina with waxed thread in an effort to ensure infection by preventing the leakage of ejaculate. The act of sewing not only relegates her to the role of diseased and excrement-filled vessel, it also prevents her from reproducing. Laying claim to the maternal necessitates the ability to give life, yet Madame de Mistival is rendered a sealed container no longer able to procreate by the very act of her daughter's repudiation of their relationship.

The horror that attends Madame de Mistival's trial is evoked by the desecration of her maternal status by her daughter. Eugenie tortures her mother not only for the sake of deriving pleasure, but for the opportunity to engender herself. She becomes her own creator by annihilating the true point of her origin, which necessitates violence not only against Madame de Mistival but her womb as well.

Stay Where I Can See You!

A typically common command, this desire for the child to stay within the mother's field of vision has detrimental consequences in Coleridge's "Christabel" and Hitchcock's *Psycho*. The immediate death of Christabel's mother upon her daughter's birth prevents her from visually recognizing and accepting Christabel's newly acquired status as an other, a separate entity whose life is no longer physically intertwined with her own. The characterization of Geraldine and Christabel's post-coital slumber (the nature of which expels Christabel from her wombed-in existence) as "still and mild, / As a mother with her child" (ll.300-1)[8] emphasizes the importance of the inevitable moment in which the mother sees the child's individual being. Prior to Geraldine's arrival, the mother attempts to maintain the permanent possession of her child by enclosing her within a wombed-in world, signified by the constant darkness and Christabel's lack of tactile experience with others, who can only be characterized by their absence. This consequently jeopardizes the well-being of Sir Leoline, who has been rendered impotent and prevented from engaging in a system of exchange that would allow him to give Christabel to a man who could in turn help to re-vitalize the kingdom. The mother's prolonged possession demands the intervention of Geraldine, who must devour the devouring mother and sexually contaminate Christabel in order to achieve the latter's expulsion. Christabel's own fascinated gaze upon Geraldine's deformity signifies a desire to know the nature of Geraldine's mark, the realization of which can only be contaminatory. The injunction barring any speech that seeks to reveal Geraldine's true serpentine nature is enforced by the mark's shocking appearance, which defies description and intimates the yet to be articulated prohibition of speech. Due to Christabel's lack of experience with the immediacy of vision, which in itself compromises her command of language and its proper significations since it is through vision that one typically comes to name objects, she can only absorb and internalize Geraldine's true nature, the likes of which dictate her behavior. Without the capacity to name what one sees, the act of which can determine one's relationship to the object in question, a division between self and other fails to be established, and what is not other must, therefore, be I. In the unusually bright light of the morning after, Christabel is subjected to a barrage of images unmediated by the darkened environment, the likes of which afforded refuge to even the narrator who falls into silence ("A sight to dream of, not to tell" [ll.253-4]), the verbal equivalent of looking away upon Geraldine's disrobing. It is a sight that can only be negotiated in the dream, a realm that escapes literalization, where meaning is predominately derived through possible interpretations of a metaphor. The very secrecy of Christabel and Geraldine's liaison further exacerbates the preclusion of any accurately spoken word.

Christabel's expulsion from the womb is also the expulsion from its privileging gaze, a center of attention in which only she is of importance, one within which she is as much protected as she is confined. Once re-born out into the world, however, she gains the capacity to be seen, thus, allowing another's gaze to bestow her with object status, especially in light of her inexplicable behavior. Such status leaves her vulnerable to rejection, as evidenced by Leoline's act of turning away from her. Caught in the gaze of Geraldine she cannot verbally communicate the truth of the other's nature and in the look from her father she and the death-like atmosphere that have pervaded the kingdom are rejected, replaced in his favor by Geraldine.

The Baron relegates Christabel to the role of spectator, and as such is confined to the act of observing the interaction between Geraldine and her own father. The passivity that attends this role bars any active participation/interference on the part of Christabel. She becomes an impotent eye, one whose look means nothing to those upon whom it rests, one that requires no acknowledgement. Her disappearance from her father's field of vision also extends to that of the reader, whose eyes never see mention of her name again for the remainder of the poem. Christabel becomes absent from the text itself only to be anonymously alluded to in the form of a sexually ambivalent child whose father's love can only be evidenced by his cruelty.

Unlike Christabel's mother who seeks to re-internalize her child, Mrs. Bates gives birth to Norman only to re-claim him as a vessel in whom she may maintain her own existence. Norman's failure to find peace within Mother's excessive gaze not only leads to her murder but also to the re-articulation of an even more all-encompassing maternal gaze. Norman's existence, having been situated and validated in the eyes of his mother, demands that he maintain the illusion of her existence if his own is to be given any meaning. His predilection for taxidermy further emphasizes the desperation with which he attempts to remain the object of his mother's gaze, the potency of which is purposefully weakened by its dissemination through the many stuffed birds that surround him. This peripheral world away from which the highway has been moved (Norman's lament and explanation for the constant vacancies in the motel) functions not only as his home, but also as a sphere within which Mother exerts her influence even in death.

Despite Norman's attempt to assert himself by poisoning her, he remains within her control, the extent of which is testified to by his linguistic ineptitude. Mother, whose gaze bestows value upon and confirms Norman's existence in an otherwise unseen and "inaccessible" world to outsiders, is also the cause of Norman's discomfort with language. Aware that he is indeed being watched, he approaches conversations with others as if his very words were under surveillance as well. Although language for Norman is the means by which he controls Mother, it also confines the very content and intention of his words, as evidenced by the repetitions which attend their discussions. Because he shares his voice with Mother, it functions as a "life-giving" commonality the nature of which renders it difficult for him to conceal whatever he may say to anyone. It is as if his voice became the means by which Mother hears. Such linguistic "vulnerability" is exploited by Mother, whose growing power becomes signified by an alien eloquence and inflection which intermittently dominate Norman's own voice. Thus, the progression toward a more sophisticated linguistic structure, away from the stuttering and repetition, indicates Mother's increasing hold upon Norman, which is seemingly made permanent by her disembodied declaration, "I'm Norma Bates!"—an irreversible possession ominously enforced by her look into the camera.

In "Christabel" and *Psycho*, language and vision are intricately bound in a manner indicative of heightened tensions which attend what can only be characterized as the attempt of the maternal to subjugate and possess her child, at the cost of the child's own psychological well-being. *The Bacchae* and *Philosophy in the Bedroom* concern themselves more with physical violation that results in fragmentation/dismemberment and mutilation, all of which appear to reject the wholeness behind which the body and the mind masquerade.

The rejection, however, is a consequence and indictment of the inadequacy of words, which fail to express and negate that potential deceitfulness of sight—an always already unsuccessful attempt to overcome the impressions of vision with verbal truths. Agave's maternal gaze fails to affirm Pentheus' identity and in so doing strips away the fiction that attends the mirror stage, the actual success of which establishes "that illusion of fullness and presence by imaging the self as a unified body."[9] This in turn becomes literalized in the destruction of Pentheus' body. As in de Sade, the corporeal form which ordinarily serves to perpetuate the fiction of psychological wholeness must be fragmented if it is to finally testify to the truth: that it has been no more than the site of displacement, the evidence for denying that an accurate representation of one's lack of self/identity cannot be achieved. The belief that one can fully know one's self validates the notion that one can rely and trust one's perceptions about others. In the figure of the mother, this belief becomes particularly problematic, for she not only applies this same misconception to herself but to her relationship with her child as well. The intimacy of pregnancy physically links mother and child so that the latter functions as an extension of the former, thus collapsing any perspectival distance. The significance of the fragmented corporeal form cannot be withstood by those who understand its implications. The truth can only be tolerated temporarily, thus demanding that the body be "restored." Pentheus' scattered limbs and bones must, therefore, be gathered together once again. His very head presented by his mother heralds the identity of what would have otherwise been anonymous body parts. For Geraldine, the possibly temporary transformation of her physical deformity and restoration to vitality demand Christabel's realization of her own lack of subjective completion through an incapacity to linguistically convey what she has seen. The adage "seeing is believing" is of particular resonance for it speaks to the unquestionable acceptance of what one believes to be the truth through sight, the likes of which silence the need for language.

Notes

1. Interestingly enough it is usually disease which can distinguish the appearance of one eye from another. Cataracts cause a clouding of the eye's lens. Corneal diseases, of which "pink eye" is one, may result in a tearing or redness of the cornea. There are even ocular herpes which carry the connotation of sexual disease despite the condition resulting more often from the herpes associated with cold sores than those communicated through more venereal means—an apropos "consequence" of Achilles Tatius' view of the eye as sexually empowered. See Achilles Tatius, *Leucippe and Clitophon* in *Collected Ancient Greek Novels,* trans. John J. Winkler, ed. B.P. Reardon (Berkeley: University of California Press, 1989), 170-284.

2. It is only because the pupil is small and understated that I am comfortable with looking into it. With the invention of color contacts, people are now able to have any eye color they so desire. I am discomforted by eyes without irises, and these often appear in cinema to signify the inhuman. The most shocking part of the musician Marilyn Manson's appearance is the yellow contact that he wears in his eye because that particular color is not only "unnatural" but also recedes into the whiteness of his eyeball which, in turn, produces a black void in the center. In the movie *The Stepford Wives* (1975), the robot eyes remain completely black in the face of the original; only when the latter is destroyed can the former's eyes take on color. In *The X-Files* (1998), aliens infect humans with a black tar-like virus that works its way through the body, eventually discoloring the eyes into blackness.

3. In *Visual and Other Pleasures*, a compilation of Mulvey's essays, she, herself, notes the compromises she had made in order to pursue particular arguments. "The articles and essays published here were not intended to last. I often sacrificed well-balanced argument, research and refinements of style to the immediate interests of the formative context of the moment, the demands of polemic, or the economy of an idea or the shape and pattern of a line of thought" (Laura Mulvey, *Visual and Other Pleasures* [London: Macmillan, 1989], Introduction, vii.) For these reasons, I tend to approach her with a degree of caution.

4. Yet the current wave of filicide cases around the world only strengthens my belief that the nature of maternal instinct as lethal is not dichotomous but actually quite universal.

5. A literal mutation would indeed reinscribe the maternal within the realm of the monstrous.

6. Euripides, *The Bacchae*, trans. William Arrowsmith, in *Euripides V: Three Tragedies*, ed. David Grene and Richmond Lattimore (Chicago, Illinois: University of Chicago Press, 1959).

7. Marquis de Sade, *Justine, Philosophy in the Bedroom, and Other Writings*, trans. and comp. Richard Seaver and Austryn Wainhouse (New York: Grove Press, 1965), 359.

8. Samuel Taylor Coleridge, "Christabel," in *English Romantic Writers*, 2nd ed., ed. David Perkins (New York: Harcourt Brace, 1995), 529-37.

9. Helga Geyer-Ryan, "Imaginary Identity: Space, Gender, Nation," in *Vision in Context: Historical and Contemporary Perspectives on Sight*, ed. Teresa Brennan and Martin Jay (New York: Routledge, 1996), 120.

Chapter One

(Re)membering to Mother in Euripides' *Bacchae*

> Can't you see me mama / Mama mama mama please / Can't you feel my heart / Can't you feel my heart / Can't you feel my heart ooh / Listen to me mama / Mama mama / You're taking away any last chances / Don't take it away / Can't you feel my heart?
>
> —*Genesis,* "Mama"[1]

Euripides' *Bacchae*, perhaps written as late in the tragedian's life as 407 B.C., has long been part of a critical tradition. R.D. Stock agrees with E.R. Dodds' assessment that *The Bacchae's* thematic and central concern is "daemonic invasion and possession."[2] For Charles Segal, the text is particularly relevant and applicable to the late twentieth century due to its primary focus upon the "dissolution of order and boundaries . . . between divinity and bestiality in man, reality and imagination, reason and madness, self and other, art and life."[3] There is no doubt that *The Bacchae* is indeed a pertinent text in the literary tradition of Greek tragedy and that it remains significant today. It is not, however, solely concerned with daemonic possession or the transgression of boundaries that compromise societal order. It is also about a character with whom we may be personally familiar, one who has often been overlooked and dismissed perhaps out of a need to avoid the possible implications of her actions.

Agave's presence in the text is not motivated by the need for a suffering character, an object of brutality that will in turn "expose the ferocity of Dionysus"[4] (the implication of which estimates her value to reside in a strictly utilitarian vein) or a woman whose actions are dictated by madness. Nor is Agave someone as foreign or exotic as the "Great Mother who pulls the son back into the orbit of her devouring power" or the Evil Mother who descends from the monstrous gorgon and savages her child.[5] Such characterizations relegate her to the realm of myth, archetypes who have lost their currency. The very extremity of these labels ought to evoke suspicion for there is more being masked than the identity of the effeminate and beardless stranger who arrives in Thebes.

The Gaze of the Maternal

The maternal gaze is characterized by a desire to re-possess a child whose existence is no longer physically bound to that of the mother. The trauma that attends the birthing of a child is indeed a rending or fragmentation of what can only be described as the maternal body at its most complete. To compensate for this loss of self (the baby is indeed part of the mother's self/narcissism), the mother privileges the visual register in that it becomes the means by which she remains "connected" to her child—space and distance are negotiated by the capacity to see the child, a visual connection becomes the surrogate for the desire to physically touch the child, thus, investing sight with palpability, one that influences and curbs the actions of a child. It is this very physicality with which sight is often characterized that explodes once the child leaves a mother's scopic field. The idiomatic expressions that accompany vision and characterize vision as informed by physical desires are acted out by the mother once her child "disappears." (Erotic vision desires consumption of the other. Maternal vision desires the re-possession of the child and it is that aspect of possession that is indeed problematic since having sprung from her body there is present an almost inalienable right to that child which motivates the mother's actions). In an effort to recuperate her own wholeness, she pursues her child in an effort to bring him/her back home despite the latter's wishes. Such an effort, however, yields disturbing consequences in the four texts which I discuss. When a mother's vision fails, the physical desires with which it has been invested take over and the touch with which the child has been nurtured becomes the means by which the child will perish.

The child is therefore born into a masquerade whose theme has been the unquestionable devotions of its mother. In the process of having been given birth, the child becomes enmeshed in a perpetual state of indebtedness that long outlasts the hours of labor. The mother wears the Dionysian smiling mask that pretends she has no desire to collect on that debt, but the eyes betray her true intention. With the removal of the mask, the nature of maternal instinct will unfortunately be revealed.

Donning the (Dionysian) Double

In *The Bacchae*, the revelation of that maternal instinct is not broached directly nor quickly for it is a truth toward which the main characters move by way of their troubled relationships. The relationship of Dionysus and Pentheus is obviously a primary and focal one. Rather than accept the god, Dionysus, Pentheus refuses until he eventually incurs the former's wrath. It is the manner in which Dionysus deals with Pentheus in the moments after he has decided the young king's fate that is most interesting. Reminiscent of D.W. Winnicott's observations regarding the manner in which a child attempts to deal with its mother's unconscious hatred,[6] Pentheus is unaware of what is happening as Dionysus prepares him for his journey to Cithaeron where the Bacchae worship. In the "truce" which the god declares with Pentheus, thus, allowing the latter to see more clearly, Pentheus becomes eager to be appropriately attired as a maenad.

His question, "Do I look like anyone? Like Ino or my mother Agave?" (ll.925-6),[7] signifies a wish to mirror a maternal figure. Pentheus' increasing compulsion to be in a sense a perfect maenad is mirrored in his concerns regarding the accidental loosening of his curls, the straightening of a skewed hemline and the proper placement of the wand in a specific hand. His desire to observe the secret rites progresses toward the desire to participate, completely unaware that he is willingly engaging in preparations for his own death:

> DIONYSUS. You and you alone will suffer for your city.
> A great ordeal awaits you. But you are worthy
> Of your fate. I shall lead you safely there;
> Someone else shall bring you back.
> PENTHEUS. Yes, my mother.
> DIONYSUS. An example to all men.
> PENTHEUS. It is for that I go. (ll.963-7)

In this short and simple exchange, Dionysus and Agave become linked in their complementary actions and in Pentheus' very words. The god and mortal mother seemingly function in concert with one another, one who brings, the other who returns, thus, perpetuating the cyclic atmosphere that characterizes the history of those involved.[8] It also, however, alludes to the cycle that begins and ends at the place of one's origin, that of the mother. And yet to depict Dionysus and Agave as complementary places them on a plane in which they are too equal. The god is in effect an escort, the one who will deliver and in a sense leave once the attack is underway. Pentheus' admission of "yes, my mother" functions both as an acknowledged identification of the one with whom he will return as well as an as an address to Dionysus *as* mother, thus implicating the maternal as the potentially overriding force. Agave herself may indeed be absent from these proceedings, but her surrogate is not.

Unique to Agave's surrogate, Dionysus, however, is his willingness and capacity to speak to Pentheus. Much of their relationship is fraught with verbal confrontations. It seems that Pentheus' ability to argue, to give voice to his own rage, beliefs, and convictions are linked to the preservation of his existence. That is, once he verbally acquiesces to the wishes of Dionysus, his own voice disappears in such a manner that both it and his physical appearance become disguised.

> DIONYSUS. You will be carried home—
> PENTHEUS. O luxury!
> DIONYSUS. Cradled in your mother's arms.
> PENTHEUS. You will spoil me.
> DIONYSUS. I *mean* to spoil you.
> PENTHEUS. I go to my reward.
> DIONYSUS. You are an extraordinary young man, and you go
> to an extraordinary experience. You shall win

> a glory towering to heaven and usurping
> god's. (ll.967-73)

Their dialogue becomes a free-flowing exchange in which Pentheus' voice and replies no longer take prominence or center stage, but recede into the background as no more than asides to an audience already dominated by Dionysus' words; to a reader whose eyes merely scan over Pentheus' mild interjections amidst the emphatic statements of Dionysus. Pentheus' voice and words become dominated by the meaning of Dionysus' own. Hollow and recessive, Pentheus' words lose their own efficacy and are manipulated by Dionysus who provides them with a destructive context within which his words are given a different and greater meaning. It is in this manner that Pentheus is last experienced directly by the audience or reader. Previously seen as a boy whose own words are so alien to himself and malleable to another, he is only to be directly encountered again as a fragment.

Pentheus' final words are reiterated by a messenger, thus emphasizing his physical disappearance and demise. The efficacy of his words is reestablished, but only in his death/absence from himself and their re-telling by another in retrospect. The present for Pentheus ceases to exist once his words are subsumed in Dionysus' own. Once this happens Pentheus disappears from the present moment inhabited by the audience. His very death is an event not to be directly witnessed but retold. For the audience there is no conclusion to the life of Pentheus, there is no death to be seen. His demise can only be accessed in the past, in the account of what the messenger had seen. In the mouth of the messenger who not only reports, but can also foretell, Pentheus becomes re-contextualized as the son whom Agave is incapable of seeing.

The disappearance of Dionysus' form in the forest is replaced by the temporary presence of his voice as if his voice is a lingering remainder of a once corporeal state that demands its speaking. His words, however, are no longer addressed to Pentheus but to the god's own followers, for Pentheus is no longer a subject but an object upon whom vengeance is to be taken. Indeed Pentheus is a man but one who becomes redefined within the parameters of an object and as such lacks the subjectivity that would demand its being addressed.

The surrogate has done what the mother will not deign to do which is to speak to the child as a subject unto himself. Pentheus' compromised subjectivity as a man via his verbal conformity and disguise transforms him into a strange object to the ones who pique his own curiosity. Dionysus' characterization of Pentheus as a "man" (l.1079) deteriorates in the words of Agave who refers to him as a "climbing beast" (l.1108), reflecting a further degradation of his status as human. He is in an abortive sense disintegrating or devolving. Once the one to whom words were spoken, he is now an object about *which* things are said. And it is in the saying that he is most threatening for Agave fears he will "reveal the secrets of the god" (ll.1108-9). The silence with which his pleas are met herald what will be the demise of a thing and a thing in itself is barred from *human* speech and, therefore, human comprehension.

In Silence There Is No Defense

Perhaps there is something to be gleaned from that old adage "children are to be seen and not heard." Often overlooked, it is a principle that relegates children to the realm of visual exposure.[9] That silence must also attend this "ideal" state bars them from speaking, from language itself—to engage in such communication is an act of defiance. The child is left to mime his wishes if he is fortunate enough to have someone watching him, but again there is an inherent powerlessness, one that renders a child an object and with as much efficacy as passivity may bestow. A great deal of weight that resides in the spoken word becomes shifted onto the act of interpretation without the presence of verbal signifiers. Why, however, would a child feel the need to negotiate such silence, a silence which is desired by the mother especially when any attempt to circumvent that wordlessness relies upon the interpretational act that by its nature is fraught with uncertainty? What exactly is at stake?

There is indeed a great deal of power that attends the status of one who is mother despite her sense of being buffeted by the whims of her child. It is she who gives meaning to the pre-verbal communications of her child, she who determines the significance of his every gesture. The infant then learns which cries and manners of behaving elicit his mother's particular responses. Their relationship becomes defined by a lack of language that further emphasizes the infant's dependency upon his mother. It is she who serves as an interpreter of his needs for others who often fail in their attempts to understand his wants. The infant cannot negotiate the world without the presence of his mother who, in turn, becomes all-encompassing.

Given this, a child's acquisition of language provides a more unmediated access to the world while limiting the mother's interpretational latitude. It is a step toward independence for the child since his words are invested with meanings that must be taken into account. His ability to speak forces the mother into another realm of communication that may at times demand she justify her actions to the child whereas prior to this there was no need. Intuition no longer suffices as a "reasonable" validation for her actions concerning her child—now she is confronted by the possibility of having to reason and explain to a being who "belongs" or is "of" her both of which imply redundancy and insult. The confidence in the maternal sphere of influence in which the child resides becomes suspect. The mother's sense of security in her possession or ownership of her child is compromised in that moment of having to decide whether or not to answer her child, in that moment of *questioning* that demands her *response*. The bond between them, born of silence is compromised by the child's emergence into language. In order to reestablish the power dynamic of active speaker (mother) and passive listener (child) which the child is now threatening to disrupt, she must annihilate the very desire in the child to speak. The latter's verbal inquiry is therefore met with the gaze of the maternal: that which responds within the very absence of language and relegates the child to a state of infancy when the child was incomplete. It is in a sense a momentary severing of the capacity to speak from its desiring within the child.

The refusal to condescend to providing a response can be mentally justified by a claim that a child is incapable of understanding the possible reasons that would be given to his inquiries. This in effect is a way of ignoring the child and again imposing limitations upon him as he once had been limited by the absence of language, by the confines of the maternal body. It is therefore proper that the mother respond with no more than a look, that which operates on the level of silence, a refusal to engage within the linguistic realm to which the child now has access. The mother's look evokes a time prior to language when the child's needs were communicated without words. That look conveys a superiority, a moment in which the child is reminded of his own ineffectuality as a human being in the face of one who remembers his inarticulate primitivism and that in itself is enough to render the child mute once again. In the look of the mother, the child's own gaze becomes absorbed, appropriated, and turned back upon the child, causing him to see himself as an object, as a thing. In turn this has a splitting or alienating effect upon the child for he occupies two spaces at once: that of subject (seeing) and object (being seen), or in other words, he sees himself seen. This is a breakdown of boundaries which typically serve as protection for the child's sense of self, boundaries that have been formulated with the aid of the mother who in her involvement also (however subconsciously) knows the child's weaknesses. For the child who speaks but is met with silence, the need for another to return his words is left unfulfilled and renders him incomplete, waiting to have his own words acknowledged. Providing his own response is an act that he himself is barred from doing since to do so marks one as mentally unstable because it requires a splitting within the subject, thus the need for another is built in. The consequence of attempting to circumvent the role of the other in such a dialogue calls Norman Bates to mind who suffers from his own psychic splitting and eventual annihilation of not only his own voice but his own being.

Language for the child may very well be the means by which he attempts to forget how inhuman he once was while simultaneously attempting to assert his autonomy from the mother. Thus it is through the mouth that the child not only gains nourishment but defends against the impositions of a mother's capacity to think of the child solely in relation to herself rather than to himself as an individual. The opportunity to defend himself is in the linguistic emanations of the mouth or in the expulsion of words that can challenge the authority of the mother over her child. As much as one may take into the mouth (food), one may also expel but note that what is tangibly ejected is often in the form of vomit, a rejection or wasting of food. In the case of Pentheus, his words overwhelmingly express the sentiment of rejection and in the face of Agave those too are wasted.

"I'm So Hungry I Could Eat You": The Secret of Maternal Instinct

The capacity to see the child as less than human (assuming that language is a defining factor) or as a thing/object, results in his vulnerability at the hands of his mother who due to the nature of their relationship is, biologically speaking, the one most vested with proprietary rights. Since it is my contention that maternal vision is informed by a desire to figuratively re-possess the child and that once the capacity to see becomes compromised, the maternal seeks possession in more tangible and destructive ways, I must turn for a moment to D.W. Winnicott: "[W]hereas all babies take in food, there does not exist a communication between the baby and the mother except in so far as there develops a mutual feeding situation" (Winnicott, 255). It would thus appear that within the mother-child relationship communication and the act of feeding which guarantee the "cross-identification" (Winnicott, 256) that ensures the child's well-being are inextricable so much so that the child feeds at the breast of one who will come to desire its devouring, a desire that lurks in the very posture assumed in the feeding scenario.[10] The natural position in which the mother feeds her infant is one that attempts to protect, to create a feeling of safety by enveloping. Enveloping, however, necessitates the surrounding or collapsing of another *into* oneself which in this case, and if need be, would allow the maternal body to "reconfigure" itself as the womb within which the infant once lodged. It is certainly a posture of possession, of re-forming boundaries, of preventing access to the infant in order to protect possibly at the expense of the mother's own physical harm. There is always in that very posture a promise of maternal self-sacrifice which given the eventual expectations of a child by its mother appears to attend the "mutuality" of the feeding situation. For Winnicott, the mother is able to adapt to the infant's needs because she is able to identify with having been an infant (Winnicott, 256); that in itself requires that she resituate her subjectivity within that of the infant's. This compromises the already tenuous distance/recognition between self and other, for in sharing a subjectivity the infant is made even more into herself, to a seeing out of or perhaps a peering into one's own eyes to determine the needs of another. That mutuality, that maternal capacity to make real what the infant requires is a literalizing component epitomized by the act of breastfeeding. Once the infant is weaned, however, the maternal body does not retain the same signification to the child as it once had. The maternal body instead becomes obsolete for it is no longer home (womb) nor direct source of nourishment.

Unable to feed off of the child as the child had fed at her breast, the desire to devour becomes retranslated or re-formed into a desire to possess, a lesser and more insidious passion. The means by which this new desire will attempt its satisfaction, but fail, is through that of sight. Incapable of physically connecting with the child as she once had, she is also now barred from the *possibility* of enveloping it that resides within and characterizes the posture of feeding. It is the existence of that very possibility that maintains a sense of security and dominance in the mother over her child. Without that possibility to possess which is made real in the act of feeding, the mother must then resituate herself within the realm of the figurative if she is to maintain/match that prior sense of control over her child.

If it is no longer possible for the child to be physically possessed, the mother can figuratively engulf him within her field of vision. Maintaining the child's inclusion within her scopic field is the mother's attempt to re-possess but the impossible constancy of the child's presence jeopardizes the satisfaction of that desire. The pursuit of such a literal wish through a more figurative manner safeguards the physical well-being of the child while allowing the negotiation of the mother's wish. Without this, the safety of the child is jeopardized by the literalizing capacity of the maternal that so marked her purpose during the stages of the infant's early development. Agave's inability to acknowledge Pentheus in terms of species is in itself an act of fragmentation that precedes his physical dismemberment. The sheer failure of Agave's vision becomes compensated for by the sheer physicality of the manner in which she attacks him. Fragmentation, thus, operates first at the level of vision and then becomes literalized. The attack is then proof of two seemingly disparate ideas—his death is both testimony to Agave's psychic fragmentation that prevents her from recognizing him and perversely proof of the subtext that informs, shapes, and creeps beneath maternal vision—that desire for the physical appropriation of the child, the same desire that erupts and is achieved once maternal vision fails.

But why is the maternal desire for her child's possession so fraught with connotations of devouring? The image of the devouring mother has long been that of one in whom aspects of the beginning and the end reside, both birth and death, one who nurtures but also destroys. The relevance is located in this implication of eating and feeding, of swallowing and disappearing. The fear of this latter component is actually mirrored in the assumed posture of one who hand-feeds. The danger of which increases if it is the child who adopts a similar posture before his mother for the mother already desires his possession and re-absorption into her own self.

Linked by the act of eating, the differences between feeding and devouring must be considered. Imbedded in this idea of feeding is one who gives and one who receives, active and passive. To feed someone, that is to provide food for someone, is the means by which hospitality can be extended and hunger relieved. It signifies generosity, a willingness to nourish, and often an occasion for celebration. It expresses a concern for the other's well-being and the other's acceptance of that food indicates a trust (that the food is untainted). To devour, however, is a self-centered act characterized by greed and the absence of concern for an other. From the Latin "devorare," it is to swallow which is further suggestive of disappearance, annihilation. (Consider the many times children are admonished for having swallowed their food. The rule is to chew one's food so as to avoid choking which indicates a risk or perceived harm in the failure to do so. Yet, to swallow one's food is also bad manners for in the haste of doing so one is unable to enjoy what one is eating, the nuances of the taste are lost. One then looks at food not for its particular qualities or that which makes the meal unique but as a type of indiscernible thing whose sole purpose is to be ingested.) Thus, to devour is to consume not for the sake of nourishment but for that of destruction.[11]

Consider the manner in which the hand is poised when feeding another, when approaching the open mouth. Seldom are all fingers involved, in fact, one often takes care to involve as few as possible. "Pinching" the morsel of food between the index finger and thumb is the most common approach, following that is the added involvement of the middle finger if necessary. Whichever the case may be, the remaining digits curl inward into the palm (cases where the uninvolved fingers rigidly splay outward is often just an attempt to portray the one feeding as excessively cute or dainty). By doing so, the hand assumes a type of protective posture since the threat of an accidental bite remains—it is indeed too easy to bite or at least nip the hand that feeds. The outstretched arm itself that bridges the distance between the one feeding and the one fed also functions as a type of resistance to the complete collapsing of that distance. The arm whether completely outstretched or bent at the elbow provides for the possibility to brace oneself against another's advances. In the act of feeding another, generosity and tenderness can certainly be present, but limitations are also established in an effort to protect oneself from the other's potentially threatening mouth.

Although this is an extremely literal analysis of the handfeeding act, it is the fear of suffering some harm inflicted by the mouth that remains, and it is that mouth of the mother that signifies a swallowing up of the child, for the maternal mouth in the literal sense is the passageway to the stomach and the tomb rather than the womb for a child already expelled. It is that knowledge from which we flee, that in the very site of our origin is the threat of our being returned to the place where we once belonged. We fear our reclamation, that we will be forced to fill the space we ourselves created by our exodus. We fear the potency of our mother's desire and our own compulsion to return. As much as we were fed by our mothers in our infancy, as much as we devoured our own mother's breasts, we fear that they will collect on this debt by devouring us as well. But whereas we devoured literally they continue to do so figuratively and unceasingly. Our debt resides within that of the literal world, but what they demand is a psychic repayment.

As Pentheus screams, "No, no, Mother, I am Pentheus, / your own son, the child you bore to Echion! / Pity me, spare me, Mother! I have done a wrong /

but do not kill your own son for my offense" (ll.1117-21) *he touches her cheeks*, an often overlooked but relevant gesture on his part. And there it is, an act so simply stated and yet so laden with meaning. The simultaneity of the touch with the speaking of the words testifies to what Pentheus already knows: that the words may indeed fail to communicate his identity, that his mother will not hear him. For Pentheus, the touch with its connotations of familiarity and tenderness is his only supplement to language in the face of a mother who fails to see him. To know this is to implicate language as the primary defense against re-absorption into the mother's vision. His recourse to language is also a demand for a verbal response and to secure that is in a manner of speaking a distraction; since one cannot speak and eat at the same time, it is a tactic aimed at deferring what could be his demise. It is also an attempt to compel a contradiction among Agave's sensory perceptions. Believing she may not visibly recognize him, he hopes that his words will challenge what she sees. This disruption although his only hope is a dangerous one particularly since he seeks to fragment the perceptions of one already believed to be in a fit of madness.

The question then becomes, how does that touch fail him? What is implicit in this positioning of the hand to the cheek? Unlike the hand that feeds, Pentheus' palm is exposed, an open hand that invites. In a manner of speaking, he is summoning his mother to recognize their relationship and, on a more figurative level, for her rational mind to step forward through what appears to be madness. The very openness of his hand also signals his own vulnerability and a desire for a reply with the positioning of his arm posing no defense to any possible act of aggression by Agave. Rather than his hand touching and remaining within the boundaries of Agave's body and, thus, ensuring a surface against which to brace himself, Pentheus instead reaches for a cheek,[12] the exterior of a boundary against which one *must* slip.[13] Pentheus' gesture, rather than being met with the enveloping collapse of bodies that is an embrace (in this case signifying recognition and reunion), is instead replied with its opposite: the literal dispersion of his corporeal form. This frenzied scattering of his limbs is made more shocking by the very centrality that characterizes the scene in the forest itself. The concentricity is demonstrated by the placement of Pentheus in the tree to secure a better vantage point, the manner in which the Bacchae encircle the tree trunk in an effort to shake him down, and by the confrontation between mother and son which causes those present to "recede" into the background before re-emerging in order to dismember him.

Behind the Mask Is Just Another One

The scene in the forest is central to this text but not because it is the moment in which the audience is made to witness Dionysus' power, testified to by his ability to compel a mother to kill her own child.[14] Rather, it is the moment in which the mother emerges as the true destructive force. In the face of maternal power, even Dionysus is rendered a trope, thus, situating the divine within the agency of the mother. That Dionysus first appears clearly wearing a mask promises its removal or revelation. The smile that so characterizes it is often read as indicating the god's duality—his ability to relieve mortals' pains through drunkenness as well as an unmerciful capacity for vengeance. This latter aspect is not, however, the location of the most disturbing revelation.

The removal of the mask is announced by Dionysus himself: "Women, I bring you the man who has mocked / at you and me and at our holy mysteries. / Take vengeance upon him" (ll.1079-81). Yet he has been removed from the scene prior to even having uttered these words for his voice is heard coming from heaven. His disappearance marks the ascendancy of another, one who until this same moment has been a marginal character: Agave. The most memorable scene does not involve the god nor is the play even named for him, thus, further situating his role to the periphery. Dionysus functions instead as a trope for maternal instinct.

"I'm So Proud of Me! . . . I Mean You, Son."

In the ambiguity of Pentheus' sudden desire to be the perfect maenad whose hair remains in place under her snood, hemline lies straight, thyrsus rests in the appropriate hand, which in its raising must be accompanied by the matching movement of the foot, in the midst of this quest for the ideal are the words of the surrogate named Dionysus: "An example to all men" (l.966). In this simple phrase the maternal desire for an exemplary child is implicated. Pentheus' response, "It is for that I go" (l.967) signals the typical child's reaction to a hatred that can only be glimpsed, but seldom confirmed, understood, and even acknowledged. In the machinations of Dionysus, Pentheus can only fleetingly see the duality of the god, one that can only be known as truth, and around which Pentheus organizes his actions.[15] It is to be an example to all that Pentheus goes to the forest for it is that which will allow him to be the trophy that his mother so desires.

Rooted in the word "trope" which is a turning particularly in reference to figures of speech in which the nonliteral interpretation is privileged, the trophy is indeed a representation of a particular achievement. The same word, however, is also related to atrophy, the wasting away or deterioration of the body. The Greek root, "atrophos" is more specific in the cause of such deterioration specifying that of "ill-nourishment." By its nature, a trophy is that which turns and evokes a different meaning than the one which is alluded to on the surface and yet it signals the physical decline of a body. This decline is not represented by the trophy which instead signifies and is awarded at a moment of (often physical) accomplishment. Perhaps it is for this reason that those who wish to prove their hunting prowess often mount the heads of the animals they have killed upon their walls. It is an attempt to preserve a hunter's fleeting moment of victory. That life can be taken away from it is an aspect of its value, but that same aspect that lifelessness which renders the body a corpse with its attendant deterioration becomes that which must be kept at bay if it is to continue to serve the hunter's purpose. The illusion of animation is then lent to this head which so naturally juts out from a plaque on the wall.

Given the similarity of Agave's presentation of the "lion cub's" head,[16] a more surface-oriented interpretation would explain her actions as solely informed by her delusion. But this is too easy. Rather she wants what most mothers are unwilling to admit: praise and recognition for her triumph. "Proud and happy. / I have won the trophy of the chase, / a great prize, manifest to all" (ll.1199). Once a part of herself, only she can see the child for what his purpose is: to reflect the idealized image of her own self, hence the personalization of every shortcoming or failure of the child and the impossibility of his autonomy. This personalization is complicated by the fact that it is not merely the mother's own estimation of herself that is at stake, but her estimation in the eyes of others. The child functions similarly to that of a text which is read by others, who in turn look beyond the words and toward a sub-text that is the mother. It is then the burden of the child not only to avoid failure but to achieve some degree, some sign of greatness which in the eyes of others will testify to a mother's success. Here the value of the child does not reside in his individual person but in his capacity to double as a trophy winner. The personal desire for glory or recognition that many of us have is relinquished by the mother and replaced by the societal expectation of sheer devotion to her child (an element of what de Sade claims to be the sanctification of motherhood). In turn her natural desire for notability/admiration becomes sublimated, transferred onto the child who must achieve these things for her even at the expense of his own well-being.

In the brutality of Pentheus' death is the stark honesty of this particular desire. Agave's child is not the means to an end but what most children will never be: an end in themselves.[17] It is seldom the child of whom the mother is proud but the child's accomplishments, his capacity to achieve. The murder of Pentheus is a transformational act in that he *becomes* the inanimate trophy,[18] the very site of glory and pride for his mother—he *is* her achievement.[19] Rather than characterizing Agave and her actions as a failure or betrayal of motherhood, they are quite the opposite, for they function as testaments to the true desires of the mother.

"(Why Can't You) See What a Good Job I've Done With My Child?"

For Agave, Pentheus' death provides the opportunity for her to re-gain her memory or at least the capacity to recognize his face and her own participation in his demise. In the unbounded territory of the forest, Agave is unable to recognize Pentheus for who he is, thus implying that the status of child and the conduct exhibited toward him is not so much natural as it may be a construct of what is considered "civilization" or civilizing tendencies. Agave's natural impulses which result in Pentheus' death are so primal that her response to his pleas is in the form of pure action rather than in a linguistic register. Her silence is echoed by the "blindness" of the audience who is barred from directly witnessing her dismemberment of Pentheus, for they can only be *told* of the events. The audience is allowed to witness only the departure of the disguised Pentheus from the city and his re-introduction to Thebes as a brutalized trophy. Those moments which punctuate his actual death are barred from the theatrical scene, are never witnessed by the audience, and as such defer the audience's realization of the all too shocking truth that a mother has not only killed her child but reveled and delighted in it for the sake of her own glory.

With her arrival in the city she is questioned by the chorus to whom she proudly exhibits the head still believing it to be a lion cub: AGAVE. "See, the whelp is young and tender. / Beneath the soft mane of its hair, / The down is blooming on the cheeks" (ll.1185-87). Her awareness of the "lion's" youth is testified to by her use of the word "whelp," a word which evolves in old English to refer to the very act of birthing itself. Such reference to this fragment of Pentheus' body indicates a capacity to recognize, while the evolving definition of "whelp" reframes Agave's murderous act as a type of conception that allows her to bring forth and present this fragmented son to the world of Thebes. The implication is akin to that of an abortive gesture which in its accomplishment reflects the rending apart of the fetal body.

Underlying the imperative to "see" the whelp is a determination that must primarily be made through touch. In the tone of Agave's words to the chorus, seeing takes on a seductive quality, an invitation to touch the soft mane and blooming down that she has already felt. The murder of her son becomes tinged with a perverted beauty that she wants all to share in. Her reference to his cheeks and their accessibility to strangers mirror Pentheus' clasping of his mother's own cheek and the fruitlessness of his attempt. What she is inevitably demanding is for all to see through her own eyes, to occupy her own scopic reference, to see her child as she does: AGAVE. "The whelp of a wild lion, / And snared by me without a noose. / Look, look at the prize I bring" (ll.1173-5).[20]

Although the chorus says, "I see," Agave urges them to look as if they are not truly comprehending the status and implications of the particular prize she has brought with her. For Agave the chorus's sight is in some way deficient and unsatisfactory in its appreciation.

> CHORUS. Where was he caught?
> AGAVE. On Cithaeron—
> CHORUS. On Cithaeron?
> AGAVE. Our prize was killed.
> CHORUS. Who killed him?

AGAVE. I struck him first.
The Maenads call me "Agave the blest." (ll.1176-80)[21]

This recounting of the event is elicited by questions designed to establish responsibility for the death of the "prize." What Agave so proudly boasts having done, in actuality implicates her guilt. There is, nevertheless, an implied conflict in this exchange which is located in the use of the word, "him." In using this pronoun, the chorus evidences its knowledge of the prize not as a thing, but as a man as well as a validity in their capacity to see. Agave in responding similarly, that is, through her responsive reference of having struck/slew "him" first, betrays a vacillation in her own perception of what she carries.

There's Nothing Stronger Than a Mother's Love

The masked and effeminate stranger's true identity is not the main concern of the play, for he quickly introduces himself as Dionysus to the audience. The god's disappearance prior to Pentheus' death marks his physical form as a costume itself donned by the one whose face we are familiar with yet never truly see. Rather, it is the destructive desire of the mother with which *The Bacchae* is concerned. The play unmasks the truth of the maternal gaze, the horror of which is evoked by its failure to reside in the realm of the figurative. In the honesty of the maternal gaze, the literalizing impetus takes over and the desire to possess is recapitulated in the act of physically fragmenting its object: the child. Deferring to the future, that is, the belief that the mother will always own her child, gives way to the immediacy of the present with its attendant instant gratification. A dismembered child is better than a live one for his pieces can then be gathered in the loving arms of his mother.

Although Agave commits the crime and comes to recognize her actions, the implications of these actions in the sense that they follow traditional tragedy are comparatively marginal in what is essentially an upending of another component of tragedy. Euripides' removal of the mask signified by the literal disappearance of Dionysus from the forest reveals more than can be tolerated by theater itself. With this unmasking of true maternal instinct whose sheer desire is for the literal death of her child, there is no room for representation. What we are confronted with is an unadulterated truth that closes off any other interpretive act. Its revelation is as stunning as Pentheus' death. Agave's return to Thebes with her son's head appears to herald a conclusion for it is in doing so that the city is made to witness not only the "power" of Dionysus but also this crime of filicide so testified to by Pentheus' own head. The head held high which makes others see without its own seeing is the body part to which its fragments will soon be returned. But this is the only return that is to be had, for rather than remain within the city, Cadmus and his remaining family are cast out. Unlike her father, whose future is revealed by Dionysus[22] Agave's future remains undetermined.[23] Her expulsion from the city is an expulsion from the stage itself and like Mrs. Bates who looks into the camera and sees her audience, Agave's physical disappearance is actually her dispersion into the lives of the spectators. Inasmuch as Pentheus was physically scattered for the price of having seen, the audience must likewise pay. In their case, however, it is they toward whom Agave is dispersed. She may leave the stage but the distance between her and the spectators is not made greater, it is instead collapsed—in her existence is now the revelation that maternal instinct is naturally lethal to the child.

In the Lacanian fashion of the given-to-be-seen and the theatrical objective of the given-to-be-scene, the audience is called into existence by the spectacle. What, however, are the consequences of a spectacle that cannot be tolerated by the audience because it compromises the distance between safety and self? Do we turn away because we see ourselves reflected in the person of Pentheus, that is, as one who is at the mercy of his mother, or do we quickly deny that within the maternal resides that Agavian aspect which refuses to see what is truly there in an effort to honestly pursue and fulfill her own desires? Whichever the reason may be, the audience does look away and it is that retraction of the gaze that spells the end of theater—a consequence of theater having penetrated the audience with a gaze of its own.

Notes

1. "Mama." Words and music by Tony Banks, Phil Collins, and Mike Rutherford. © 1983 Anthony Banks Ltd., Philip Collins Ltd., Michael Rutherford Ltd., and Hit & Run Music (Publishing) Ltd. All rights controlled and administered by EMI April Music Inc. All rights reserved. International copyright secured. Used by permission.

2. R.D. Stock, *The Flutes of Dionysus: Daemonic Enthrallment in Literature* (Lincoln: University of Nebraska Press, 1989), 4.

3. Charles Segal, *Dionysiac Poetics and Euripides' Bacchae* (Princeton: Princeton University Press, 1982), 3.

4. William Arrowsmith, introduction to *The Bacchae*, by Euripides in *Euripides V: Three Tragedies*, ed. David Grene and Richmond Lattimore (Chicago: University of Chicago Press, 1959), 150.

5. Segal, 134.

6. D.W. Winnicott, *Psycho-Analytic Explorations*, ed. Clare Winnicott, Ray Shepherd, and Madeleine Davis (Cambridge: Harvard University Press, 1989), 250.

7. Euripides, *The Bacchae*, trans. William Arrowsmith, in *Euripides V: Three Tragedies*, ed. David Grene and Richmond Lattimore (Chicago, Illinois: University of Chicago Press, 1959).

8. Dionysus first appears "disguised as man, beside the stream of Dirce / and the waters of Ismenus" (Arrowsmith, ll.5-6). A cycle of familial violence and vengeance, particularly among children and maternal figures, is alluded to by the very name "Dirce," which also means "double." According to Robert Graves, Antiope is impregnated by Zeus, flees from Thebes, returns, gives birth in a thicket to sons, and is subsequently

mistreated by her aunt, Dirce. Antiope escapes from prison, seeks help from her now grown sons who had been rescued from the thicket by a cattleman. They do not recognize her, thinking instead that she is a runaway slave. Dirce arrives in a bacchic frenzy and drags Antiope away. The cattleman arrives and tells them to beware of the furies since they have failed to protect their mother. They rescue Antiope and tie Dirce by the hair to the horns of a wild bull who then kills her.

In another version of the tale, Antiope is married to Lycus who divorces her; Lycus then marries Dirce. Zeus impregnates Antiope, but Dirce suspects Lycus is the father. Dirce imprisons Antiope who is freed by Zeus in time to give birth to twins. After they are grown, Antiope persuades them to avenge the wrongdoings of Dirce. They meet Dirce on the slopes of Cithaeron in a bacchic frenzy and tie her by the hair to the horns of a wild bull. When she is dead they fling her body on the ground where a spring wells up. Dionysus avenges the death of his worshipper by sending Antiope into a mad rage, roaming through Greece until she is cured by a grandson of Sisyphus and married.

Ismenus refers to one of Niobe's seven sons, the rest of whom were murdered by Apollo while Niobe's daughters were killed by Artemis, for Niobe's presumption that she and her children were better than Leto who had borne Apollo and Artemis. For nine days and nights, no one would bury the bodies because Zeus had turned the Thebans into stone. On the tenth day, the Olympians themselves conducted the funerals. Niobe fled, and Zeus, pitying her, turned her into a statue.

Acteon, Pentheus' cousin, is destroyed by his own hounds who believe him to be a deer after spying on Artemis. Both he and Pentheus seem to be subject to this transposition of the animal image. See Robert Graves, *The Greek Myths* (Mt. Kisco: Moyer Bell Limited, 1988).

9. According to Winnicott, children deal with their mothers' repressed hatred by creating a false self organization characterized by exhibitions of skill designed to elicit happiness at their presence. They meet uncertainty with silence since to speak requires some degree of certainty as to what one is addressing (Winnicott, 247). Although there are slippages in language, aspects which must be interpreted, it is still the word which binds a concept, setting limitations and boundaries. Such organization does not dismiss what is actually the child's struggle to discover what is at the heart of his mother's behavior. A mother is a child's dictionary, one who continually gives meaning to what he does and says since she is the first indicator of what is not him. Despite a belief that the child is constituted not just by himself but also his environment (and of course his mother) the pursuit of her own wishes and impulses exhibits his lack of control over her, thereby proving that she is not he. What language cannot convey, the exhibition hopefully can, within the realm of sight/vision. Vision has a randomness that language does not; it is also less controllable and more instinctual than the more formal verbalization of an idea. While the gaze re-integrates and absorbs, language establishes a distance. Both are expressions of desire but with language the very word serves as a mediation; there is none with vision. Verbal silence is the equivalent to someone looking away—both compromise the existence of the other, both threaten the other with his/her own disappearance from the subject's scopic field.

10. Many infants of course are not breast-fed, yet the feeding posture remains the same.

11. It seems that the capacity to devour can also be the means of impregnation. Zeus, in an attempt to circumvent a prophecy which stated that Metis, already pregnant with a female child, would eventually bear a boy who would depose Zeus, swallowed her. After some time, he was seized with a headache and from his head sprung Athena fully armed.

Cronus, Zeus' father, had earlier swallowed all of his children in an effort to avoid a similar prophecy. Zeus was hidden from Cronus who was instead given a stone in the baby's place and promptly swallowed that as well. In the war which eventually followed, Zeus poisoned his father which caused him to vomit out his siblings: Hestia, Demeter, Hera, Hades, Poseidon.

12. In another translation of *The Bacchae*, Pentheus is said to touch "her cheek" (Euripides, *The Bacchae,* in *Ten Plays by Euripides*, trans. Moses Hadas and John McLean [New York: Bantam Books, 1981], 306), whereas Arrowsmith reads "cheeks." The latter implies that Pentheus would have used both hands, one to each side of his mother's face. Given this, he is in a sense holding her head which is perversely reflected in Agave's carrying of his head. Both instances of holding are in opposition to one another: one signifying life, the other death, the intact body as opposed to the dismembered one. Touching both cheeks increases the urgency of the situation in that it is often an act of desperation and coercion, a physical demand to make one focus or concentrate rather than to allow one to look away.

13. It is the language of the cheek to be caressed. Any child who has had his/her cheeks pinched will agree with that.

14. If taken as a testament to Dionysus' power, the mother-child bond is a highly esteemed one particularly in light of this filicide as a warranted response to the blasphemies and wrong-doings levied against a god. The murder of a child at the hands of its mother becomes the moral equivalent to an offense against divinity. These transgressions (blasphemy against gods and the shedding of kindred blood) are also among those punished by the Furies or Erinnyes (punishment for a third offense, the violation of host/guest rules is also allotted to them).

15. A mother's unconscious hatred due to its nature cannot be directly accessed, realized, or voiced in words by her since she herself remains unaware to some degree. According to Winnicott, such moments of hatred are simultaneously accompanied by tenderness (Winnicott, 250). The child in turn responds primarily with exhibitions of skill rather than words (Winnicott, 247-8). This false sense of self is mirrored in Pentheus' drastic cross-dressing.

16. According to Winnicott, "not being able to talk has a curious effect in that it demands a listening which is different from my ordinary way of listening. To some extent I always listen with my throat, and my larynx follows the sounds that I hear in the world and particularly a voice of someone talking to me" (Winnicott, 83). Although Agave is said to have "pick[ed] up [Pentheus'] head, / [and] impaled it on her wand" (Arrowsmith, 1140-1), Graves writes that it was indeed she who "wrenched off" his head (Graves, 105). The nature of such an act is violence primarily against the neck since it is this which must be severed if no more than the head is to be secured. This particular location, thus, includes an attack against the throat. Given Winnicott's view, if the larynx shares the same function as an ear that listens to the world and particularly the voice of one talking to him, then severing the throat has a dual consequence: that of deafening as well as silencing/muting the other. This is a transformative act that renders a corporeal fragment into a trophy. During wartime, heads are known to be impaled and prominently displayed as signs of victory, warning, or an assertion of power.

17. A child's value is in its utility and malleability. There is always a greater significance attending the decision to have a child, that is, one does not have a child for its own sake but for the parent's own (i.e., the desire to pass on the family name, the fear of not being cared for in old age, a wish to achieve a sense of fulfillment, an attempt to defeat

one's own mortality, etc.). Strangely enough, those who choose not to have children are characterized as selfish.

18. Pentheus' head is more than what is outwardly expressed as well as a stark confrontation with the body that has declined so drastically it is no longer whole but a fragment.

19. My envious tone is not imagined, thus testifying in some degree to Winnicott's observations.

20. The translation by Hadas and McLean reads, "Without a noose I snared it—the young whelp of a savage lion. Look and see" (Hadas and McLean, 307).

21. The translation by Hadas and McLean reads, "Chorus: From where in the wilds? / Agave: Cithaeron / Chorus: Cithaeron? / Agave:—Slew him. / Chorus: Who was she who smote him? / Agave: Mine was the first honor. 'Happy Agave' they call me in the revel" (Hadas and McLean, 307). In *The Bacchae* edited by T.A. Buckley, "Chorus: From what desert? / Agave: Kithairon— / Chorus: Kithairon? / Agave: slew him. / Chorus: Who struck him? / Agave: The honor is mine first. I am called blessed Agave in the revels" (ll.1176-80). Euripides, *The Bacchae*, *The Perseus Digital Library,* ed. T.A. Buckley. www.perseus.tufts.edu/cgi-bin/ptext?doc=Perseus%3Atext%3A1999.01.0092 (1 July 2001).

22. Dionysus reveals that Cadmus' trials will come to include ravaging many cities, sacking a shrine to Apollo, and expiating for that crime. In the end, however, he and Harmonia are to be saved by Ares (Arrowsmith, ll.1330-9).

23. According to Graves, Agave eventually murders her husband, Lycotherses, the King of Illyria, in whose kingdom she had sought sanctuary after Pentheus' death. Agave then gives the kingdom to Cadmus who has been commanding the Enchelean forces in opposition to Lycotherses (Graves, 199).

Chapter Two

A Breast to Dream of, Not to Tell: Re-birth in "Christabel"

> Who has not watched a mother stroke her child's cheek or kiss her child *in a certain way*, and felt a nervous shudder at the possessive outrage done to a free solitary human soul?
>
> —*John Cowper Powys*[1]

Readers of Coleridge's "Christabel" are often intrigued by its strangeness and fragmentary nature which are introduced within the frame of a poem characterized by overtones of a gothic fairy tale. A young maiden leaves her father's castle to pray in the forest for the welfare of her betrothed knight who is far away. She promptly discovers a woman in distress, offers her protection, and spends the night with her only to discover that the strange woman bares a shocking deformity. She is then subjected to a spell which prevents her from telling the truth and causes her to exhibit signs of odd behavior, the severity of which compels her father to reject her in favor of this newcomer. The woman, whose mark has since disappeared, walks off with the maiden's father, and the tale ends.

On its surface, the poem may be interpreted as primarily concerned with a force of evil assailing the virtue and innocence of an unsuspecting girl, but this in itself is as unsatisfying as Coleridge's unfinished ending. The eroticism which characterizes Christabel and Geraldine's one evening together, although important, is also one which overshadows other aspects of the poem, such as the transgressive quality which attends Christabel's own behavior as well as the desires of her deceased mother. It is indeed her mother who sets events in motion by insisting upon encasing Christabel within a wombed environment that necessitates the arrival of a strange and mysterious figure—one with the capacity to silence another with a shifting of her eye.

Maternal Manifestations

Although the poem preliminarily alludes to the presence of a masculine force, the world inhabited by Christabel is not governed by the paternal. It is instead an existence marked by signs of a deceased mother who has translated the maternal bond into one of proprietary ownership of her only child. Despite her death, the figure of the mother remains inescapable.

> Sir Leoline, the Baron rich,
> Hath a toothless mastiff bitch;
> From her kennel beneath the rock
> She maketh answer to the clock,
> Four for the quarters, and twelve for the hour;
> Ever and aye, by shine and shower,
> Sixteen short howls, not over loud;
> Some say, she sees my lady's shroud. (ll.6-13)[2]

The belief that the mastiff may see the mother's ghost links the world of the living to the dead; the link, however, is established not through "ordinary" sight, but sight that is unavailable to human experience. This "camaraderie" between the mastiff and spirit is as much a consequence of their respective status as mothers as it is an abandonment/separation from their offspring, however unwillingly it may have occurred. Christabel's mother dies in childbirth, and, therefore, becomes physically unavailable to her daughter, while the dog's characterization as a bitch implies that she, too, has offspring but whose existence is not the concern of the text. Both seem to allude to the inevitability of separation between mother and child, but the situation concerning Christabel is one bearing the mark of the premature.

The stanza is characterized by the concealment of the maternal, of one who is present though not necessarily seen, the proliferation of which implies an impropriety. This "hidden-ness" is further highlighted by the idea that the mastiff only sees a sign of the mother (the shroud) which in itself implies a double function. Used to wrap and protect the dead body, the shroud further emphasizes this need to hide the body from sight that is not just human; it is as if its placement in the ground must also go unrecognized by nature itself. This protective function of the shroud may speak to the mother's wish to protect her only daughter, but it becomes subverted by an on-going effort to extend her burial cloth over the living body of Christabel.

However apropos it may be for the mother to forge a bond with the mastiff, since it is the latter's function to protect the inhabitants of the castle and her nature as a maternal figure that would compel her to guard Christabel in particular, the mastiff is not without some telling limitations. Her toothlessness juxtaposes what was once formidable protection with what is now impotent and rendered useless. Her "answers" (l.9) to the clock emphasize an awareness of the passing of time, the marks of which she bears. Although the mastiff may be in the service of the mother, the former's ineffectuality will later characterize the spirit's own efforts to "protect" her child.

Upon Geraldine's entry into the castle, the mastiff uncharacteristically moans: "The mastiff old did not awake, / Yet she an angry moan did make! / And what can ail the mastiff bitch? / Never till now she uttered yell / Beneath the eye of Christabel" (ll.147-51). In this and the previous stanza, the word, "beneath" functions as an introduction to a dichotomy in meaning, one that concerns the seen and unseen and the very tension that accompanies this vacillation. "From her kennel beneath the rock" (l.8) and "Beneath the eye of Christabel" (l.151) emphasize a duality in meaning that attaches itself to this particular word depending upon the nature of its object. "Beneath" when used with words to which no light-giving function is associated, connotes concealment and secrecy—the fact that the mastiff's shelter is under a rock emphasizes her invisible embeddedness within the very foundation of the castle. The invocation to concealment is also found in Christabel's effort to suppress and hide her fear upon hearing Geraldine's low moan by "fold[ing] her arms beneath her cloak" (l.55). However, "beneath" when used with those words that are associated with light, the meaning which is conveyed shifts into the exact opposite: that which is made visible. The mastiff senses danger but in her sleep can only moan in anger and futility, the act of which stems from an ability to detect the unseen danger that attends Geraldine's arrival. This danger is further emphasized by the fact that it has never before expressed any anger within Christabel's presence, a presence that becomes re-articulated as an "eye" and defined by the scope of her gaze. Such a tenuous and virtually intangible existence, by extension of this trope, resists containment since the world within which she resides is further fraught with other unseen and absent figures. Christabel's inability to visually perceive others is a limitation juxtaposed with the mastiff's keen perception, which also serves as a link between the dog and Geraldine, the only other figure capable of discerning the spirit's presence. Given Geraldine's serpentine characteristics, animal vision becomes not only more "insightful" than that of human, but also more powerful.

The moon maintains an equally tenuous presence, the likes of which indicate a reluctance to see: "The thin gray cloud is spread on high, / It covers but not hides the sky. / The moon is behind, and at the full; / And yet she looks both small and dull" (ll.16-9). The imagery, that of a heavy-lidded eye with the thin cloud functioning as an eyelid and the moon in its smallness similar to a pupil, indicates an event that the moon does not care to witness and, instead, seeks to shield itself from as if already aware of what is about to transpire.[3] Nature is situated as a force that reluctantly agrees with what will happen by limiting its own scope of vision in an effort to avoid complicity in Christabel's downfall. The fact, however, that the moon is indeed a participant signifies an attempt to correct an imbalance which has been detrimental not only to Christabel and Leoline, but also to progress itself. That the moon is characterized as "small" and "dull" (l.19) is a link to Geraldine's serpentine eye which "blinks dull and shy" (l.583). The shared similarities support the idea that both are working in collusion to defeat/banish the mother's spirit, as if her attempt to "own" Christabel has upset a balance between maternal forces and the dictates of nature, both of which are not only unified in the figure of the moon, but also demand the child's expulsion into the world of knowledge and the end of innocence as signified by the serpentine Geraldine.

Once Geraldine enters Christabel's bedroom, the moon attempts to repress the knowledge of forthcoming events: "The moon shines dim in the open air, / And not a moonbeam enters here" (ll.175-6). The moon's reluctance to shine so much as a beam into the room, may allow it to forget as well as negate its own complicity, the necessity of which is demanded by her traditionally maternal nature. The moon takes refuge in that causal connection between vision and the reality of occurrence—by refusing to witness the "union" between Christabel and Geraldine, the expectation for her intervention becomes nullified especially since light tends to threaten Geraldine's masquerade. The moon's desire to remove itself betrays not only its ambivalence but also its own helplessness.

The Wasteful Womb

Christabel lives a wombed-in existence, one that is enclosed and sedentary where experience is filtered and sterile. The presence of boundaries speaks to an effort to constrict her movement and her knowledge of this is evidenced by the silence with which she subsequently transgresses them. The reality of Christabel's world becomes even more questionable by the sheer absence of tactile interaction with others. Aside from the death of her mother, her "betrothed knight" (l.28) is far away and his fate unknown while Leoline, her father, has remained sick and in bed. Each one is a visually unverifiable presence with whom immediate physical contact has been barred.

The forest is a virtual wasteland in which re-birth and re-awakenings have been stifled, an environment being drained of life. Inasmuch as the womb serves a nurturing and propagating function, it also has the capacity for the obverse. It is not in the nature of the womb to be permanently occupied, that is, at the end of the gestation period during which the child is allowed to feed off of the mother's resources, there must be an expulsion or separation. To prolong this, or to encase the child within the same parameters of a womb, invites the maternal to engage in a reverse parasitic relationship since a symbiotic one is impossible. The internalization of one demands that its needs be met by the other.

Although it is "a month before the month of May" (l.21), springtime approaches slowly and with great reluctance: "And naught was green upon the oak / But moss and rarest mistletoe" (ll.33-4). The appearance of "rarest mistletoe," that whose very presence bespeaks an anomaly, evidences this condition of waste and attaches itself to the colorless oak tree. The etymology of mistletoe "stems from an Indo-European root 'meigh' which means 'to urinate,' and which also produces 'micturate.'"[4] This fluid waste, however, cannot withstand absorption, and it is in this manner of disappearance that the mother's spirit will eventually be defeated. Because mistletoe is also parasitic by nature, there remains a threat of infection if it remains. The maternal then becomes a condition which must, like urine, be discarded, a sadeian by-product whose retention serves no purpose.

This colorless world is overshadowed by the very presence of Geraldine whose initial circumvention of the maternal is signified by her appearance on the other side of a "huge, broad-breasted, old oak tree" (l.42). The difficulty she encounters at the gate "that was ironed within and without" (l.127) signifies her entrance not just into the castle but into a world in which she does not belong. This double-ironed gate signifies an oppressiveness that evidences a willingness to bar the enemy at the expense of confining its own inhabitants. Geraldine's appearance in the forest implicates this area as a weak and ill-guarded perimeter, and one, therefore, prohibited to Christabel, thus explaining the latter's need for stealth as she leaves the castle.

Christabel, whose prayer for the welfare of her lover and her own protection seems to initiate the arrival of Geraldine, elicits a sadeian response. Rather than the prayer serving as a wish for protection and salvation, it functions as an invitation to harm. It is this wish for divine intervention and aid, the likes of which are reiterated by the narrator himself, that instigates more harmful acts as if to prove not only the uselessness of a god, but the absence of one as well. Christianity in particular is referenced throughout this poem because it is the means by which the maternal becomes sanctified,[5] and the foundation upon which the mother's spirit is given preferential ownership of the child which manifests itself in this closed-off system of existence. For Geraldine to appear must, therefore, be at the behest of an even higher and more mysterious power.

> There she sees a damsel bright,
> Dressed in a silken robe of white,
> That shadowy in the moonlight shone:
> The neck that made that white robe wan,
> Her stately neck, and arms were bare;
> Her blue-veined feet unsandal'd were;
> And wildly glittered here and there
> The gems entangled in her hair.
> I guess, 'twas frightful there to see
> A lady so richly clad as she—
> Beautiful exceedingly! (ll.58-68)

Christabel fails to trust the visual strangeness of Geraldine, that uncanniness which first elicits a plea of "Mary mother, save me now!" (l.69). This initial fear is wrought by Geraldine's disquieting abundance that simultaneously attracts and repulses, the effect of which will be illustrated by Christabel's fascinated gaze as Geraldine disrobes. Her excessive beauty is on the cusp of an indescribable ugliness, as if she occupies that pinnacle of fecundity on the verge of decay. It is a moment in which the cohabitation of such extremes emphasizes the intimacy of life and death within a single body, an inherent wasting away from which there is no protection. Christabel's gesture of reaching out to Geraldine, an act which the latter must prod her to do, also functions as acceptance to progress toward knowledge rather than remaining within this state of maternally enforced innocence.

Geraldine's reluctance to pray is based upon the status of the one to whom Christabel desires her to do so: "Praise we the Virgin all divine / Who hath rescued thee from thy distress! / Alas, alas! said Geraldine, / I cannot speak for weariness" (ll.139-42). The figure of the Virgin Mary is particularly problematic for Geraldine given her directive to expel Christabel from her wombed-in existence. As one sent to banish a mother's spirit, Geraldine cannot possibly pray to the most sanctified of mothers. This religious icon conceives a child without the need for sexual intercourse, an idea that life can be propagated without the loss of sexual innocence. The very status of a virgin is an annihilating one if not discarded since its preservation will not tolerate the perpetuation of the human race. The virgin is an ideal whose womb is purposefully wasted by being barred from the possibility of engendering life. Geraldine is indeed the antithesis of the virgin figure whose appearance is anything but demure, and whose supposed circumstance, a maiden seized by five warriors, introduces the element of sexual violation.

Transgressive Substitutions

Geraldine's shifting role is one that complicates any definitive characterization of her. Suffering and helpless one moment, but triumphant and tormenting the next, she can only be defined as transgressive. The range of personas she exhibits to Christabel collapses a lifetime of experiences into one evening that expels Christabel out of a confining innocence.

Geraldine's initial appeal is in the voice of a helpless and ravished maiden whose safety remains in jeopardy. By doing so, she secures Christabel's aid and comfort.

> O well, bright dame! may you command
> The service of Sir Leoline;
> And gladly our stout chivalry
> Will he send forth and friends withal
> To guide and guard you safe and free
> Home to your noble father's hall. (ll.106-111)

Christabel's response, however well-meaning, is also indicative of one whose own sense of self does not necessarily conform to her identity as a maiden as much as it does to that of a young man. Her appropriation of masculine manners and words situates her not as the daughter of a baron but, initially, as the baron himself. By claiming that Geraldine "command[s] / the service of Sir Leoline" (ll.106-7), there is a linguistic mis-reference to the true speaker, that is, without the narrative clarification of Christabel as the speaker, one would risk mistaking the owner of those words. The use of the possessive pronoun in "our stout cavalry" (l.108) indicates Christabel's dominant affiliation with the masculine and emphasizes the degree to which she has usurped the privileges relegated to men. The tragic perversity, however, attends this very promise of refuge and safety for Geraldine. By pledging her father's protection, Christabel bars herself from later speaking against Geraldine, since to do so would compromise and endanger the latter's well-being. Christabel makes a pledge, the likes of which stem from her transgressive appropriation of her father's masculine rights, that secures her father's preferential treatment toward Geraldine and prevents her from protecting herself. Moved by charity, Christabel unwittingly undermines herself and becomes complicit in her own downfall—a true sadeian victim.

In charitable fashion, Christabel requests that Geraldine "share her couch" (l.122) which is indeed an expression of a desire to comfort her guest, but amidst her masculine behavior, it takes on an odd and perverted air. In an instance when Christabel adopts a more feminine approach, it still fails to offset the masculinity that clings to her. Christabel's attempt to vanquish Geraldine's "nightmare" in a world which already seems to be plunged in sleep only propagates yet another nightmare—one that will consequently re-situate Christabel as an outcast.

Christabel's eventual ejection, this relegation to the status of one who no longer belongs, is heightened by the recollection of Geraldine's initially prohibited entrance. Her inability to cross the threshold of the gate signifies the forbidden penetration of a spiritually guarded area: "And Christabel with might and main / Lifted her up, a weary weight, / Over the threshold of the gate: / Then the lady rose again, / And moved, as she were not in pain" (ll.130-4). The "might and main" (l.130) which characterize the manner in which Christabel carries Geraldine is again indicative of a transgressive gender description since such words are traditionally linked to the strength of men. The very act of carrying Geraldine over the threshold situates Christabel as a groom[6] with his new bride while maintaining that feminine/passive and masculine/active dichotomy. The sudden disappearance of Geraldine's pain further emphasizes the need for Christabel's voluntary participation in the evening's events.

Upon reaching the door to Christabel's bedroom, Geraldine "press[es] down / The rushes of the chamber floor" (l.173-4).The emphasis placed upon this act is not only indicative of her eventual victory and the posture which Christabel will be relegated to in front of Leoline, but also signifies her entrance into the sanctuary that is at the center of the womb. The nature of the rushes which grow out of the floor, is that of a water plant, thus, suggesting the presence of a sustaining (amniotic) fluid. It is also by means of fluid that the mother's spirit is made physically present for Christabel: "O weary lady, Geraldine, / I pray you, drink this cordial wine! / It is a wine of virtuous powers; / My mother made it of wild flowers" (ll.190-3). That this is a "cordial" wine indicates its purpose is to strengthen the one ingesting it. Its Middle English meaning introduces the source of the cordial as that of the heart. The wine then contains an essence of the mother, that which informs the very nature of the wine she, herself, made while alive, and the only thing she is known to have left behind for Christabel after her death.

In this characterization of the wine as having "virtuous powers" (l.192), the mother becomes implicated in what appears to be Christabel's appropriation of the masculine. Virtue in its obvious sense refers to morality and goodness as well as chastity, particularly in women. Its archaic meaning, however, signifies manly courage and valor. Thus, the mother instigates the gender transgressions by making a wine that is "bisexually" informed. There is an unavoidable collision in meaning which seems to necessitate Geraldine's own transgression of boundaries, for she inhabits the various roles of ravished maiden, lover, mother, and daughter as if exhibiting a range of feminine facets, most of which are absent in Christabel's own "un-gendered" identity.[7] Christabel is certainly a young woman but also a virgin, a girl who has not reached womanhood through a sexual awakening and, therefore, resides more on the cusp of the male than the female as evidenced by her behavior. The absence of immediate contact with those who would contribute to the development of her female identity (lover, mother, father) leaves her neither completely masculine nor completely feminine, thus, requiring her to constantly vacillate between the two and making transgressive behavior a necessity.

The very act of drinking the wine, coupled with Geraldine's own wish for her presence ("O mother dear! that thou wert here! / I would, said Geraldine, she were!" ll.202-3), heralds the mother's arrival, or, in more applicable terms, her spirit which is also the essence of the physical body. This seemingly odd desire for the mother's presence expresses Geraldine's own reluctance to fulfill the directive, for she is not incapable of appreciating the womb as a place of relative safety and innocence. Christabel, herself, seems to denote a prelapsarian character, the cost of which appears to be an accelerated "fallen-ness" that afflicts the rest of her environment. Geraldine is, therefore, called upon to expel her from this state of existence since it is maintained not only at the expense of nature, but also progress—Leoline himself, bound to his daughter by his wife's dying prayer, has been plunged into a severe state of suspended animation from which he "may not well awakened be" (l.119).

The spirit's attempt to intervene is met by Geraldine with hostility:

> But soon with altered voice, said she—
> "Off, wandering mother! Peak and pine!
> I have power to bid thee flee."
> Alas ! what ails poor Geraldine?
> Why stares she with unsettled eye?
> Can she the bodiless dead espy?
> And why with hollow voice cries she,
> "Off, woman, off! this hour is mine—
> Though thou her guardian spirit be,
> Off, woman, off! 'tis given to me." (ll.204-13)

The mother's inability to relinquish Christabel to the world of experience and knowledge demands that Geraldine not only appropriate the desire to possess the child, bestowed upon the spirit by motherhood, but also devour the spirit, itself. By demanding the spirit "peak and pine" (l.205), Geraldine attacks the mother according to her respective states of existence: physical and spiritual. To condemn her with bodily emaciation is to denounce her as incapable of sustaining Christabel's life while also weakening the mother and child bond wrought by the sheer physicality of pregnancy. To demand she waste away from grief is an attack upon the immateriality of the spirit itself, the consequence being an obliteration of all traces of the mother.

The characterization of the mother as "wandering" (l.205) is suggestive of an aimless and potentially transgressive act of one who does not know her appropriate place. Her unseen presence, the likes of which can only be detected by Geraldine's "unsettled eye" (l.208), implies that the invisible cannot be accessed with focused vision. The eye must instead aggressively pursue these "bodiless dead" (l.209) rather than adopt the passivity that attends a focused eye. Geraldine's ability to spy the mother's presence allows the former to damn her out of an already tenuous existence.

Christabel, barred from this visual exchange, can only offer comfort by claiming that Geraldine's exposure to danger "hath *wildered*" (l.217) her. In saying so, however, she states what fails to visually resonate for her—that this characterization of Geraldine's behavior as "wildered" is etymologically rooted in a blend of words that signify wildness (*wilden*) and wandering (*wanderen*) both of which attend, and should make one suspect, her sudden appearance. It is only the reference to some unknown power that negates Geraldine's true status as wanderer, thus, allowing her to displace the mother's spirit.

The (Mis)Appropriating Eye

As Christabel and Geraldine pass through the castle in virtual darkness, the latter's ocular powers become emphasized in the "fit" (l.159) of a candle flame: "And Christabel saw the lady's eye, / And nothing else saw she thereby, / Save the boss of the shield of Sir Leoline tall, / Which hung in a murky old niche in the wall" (ll.160-3). Geraldine's eye has the power to fixate Christabel, to bar her scope of vision in a manner reminiscent of the iron gate which prevents an entrance as much as an exit. Like the mother, Geraldine is also capable of imprisoning Christabel, but her approach is a psychic barring by way of the eye. The lack of immediacy and tactile experience which seem to characterize Christabel's existence betrays a maternal concern with the physicality of the child. Her inability to privilege Christabel's psychic well-being, as shown by the former's continued sequestering of her child at the expense of her subjective identity over her physical one, speaks to a mother's initial experience of her child. Always invisible, the child within the womb can only allude to its own existence by stretching its mother's stomach. Only by looking at her own body is the mother capable of realizing the physical existence of her child, which characterizes pregnancy as inherently narcissistic. The gaze of the mother is, therefore, confined primarily to her own well-being, which by proxy testifies to that of her child's, who in turn experiences the mother as a confining space by way of the womb. Geraldine, on the other hand, attempts to instill within Christabel the desire to leave which is why it is so necessary that Christabel be, to some degree, a willing participant. Christabel must be compelled to experience that moment of birth when the child subjects its mother to its own will. It is not enough for Geraldine to devour the mother's spirit—the womb still exists as a maternal remainder out of which Christabel must emerge.

Aside from Geraldine's eye, Christabel's vision fixates upon the ornamentation rather than the shield itself. By emphasizing this particular aspect, a degree of impotence on Leoline's part seems to be suggested. The fact, however, that it is raised and privileged by Geraldine's eye implies that she seeks to restore power to its rightful (masculine) owner. The shield's function, to protect, recedes into the background as if suggesting that his duty to provide for the safety of his people has been compromised by his sickness wrought by the desires of his deceased wife. The shield trapped within a "murky old niche" (l.163) is also a vaginal image characterized by decay, which rather than promoting life, seeks to suspend it. Christabel, who aligns herself with the masculine by adopting male grammar and gestures as well as offers of protection, is also trapped within this encompassing power of an invisible mother. This moment in which Geraldine's eye and Leoline's shield become unified in Christabel's scopic field is also a glimpse into the future when the consequences of the maiden's arrival will become all too clear.

Upon greeting his daughter the following morning, he is quick to notice Geraldine's presence: "Sir Leoline, a moment's space, / Stood gazing on the damsel's face: / And the youthful Lord of Tryermaine / Came back upon his heart again" (ll.427-30). The gaze that Leoline casts upon her is so strongly informed by his desire to re-kindle a lost friendship with Roland, an old friend, that her claim to him as her father is enough for Leoline to virtually transpose their very identities. Geraldine's presence promises their reconciliation, but only at the expense of a similar alienation from his daughter. The truth is so close to the Baron that he speaks it without realizing the import of his own words because his own gaze, so compelled to re-constitute his absent friend in the figure of Geraldine, blinds him to their value.

> That they, who thus had wronged the dame,
> Were base as spotted infamy!
> "And if they dare deny the same,
> My herald shall appoint a week,
> And let the recreant traitors seek
> My tourney court—that there and then
> I may dislodge their reptile souls

From the bodies and forms of men!"
He spake: his eye in lightning rolls!
For the lady was ruthlessly seized; and he kenned
In the beautiful lady the child of his friend. (ll.436-46)

For Leoline, the severity of the wrongful act is not based upon the harm done to Geraldine herself; rather, it is determined by her relation to another of more personal importance. Her lack of intrinsic value situates her as a mode of exchange which, however objectifying that may be, will still promote progress and restore balance. As such, Geraldine promises a more immediate recuperation of a previously lost relationship than Christabel ever can since her value is linked to a sentimental affection for a deceased wife—a reunion which must, therefore, be deferred into death. Leoline's inability to further discern the meaning of the Bard's dream, by interpreting the dove as Geraldine rather than the one "call'st by thy own daughter's name" (l.533) introduces the opportunity for Christabel's eventual displacement. His visual perception characterized by an "eye [which] in lightning rolls!" (l.444) implies that he can only be moved to action by a passion fueled by rage. This tendency, however, functions as a double bind since this same rolling of the eye, by its violent and destabilizing nature, can only prevent his "focusing" upon the truth of the situation.

The Contaminated Re-birth

Christabel's initial birth is one that occurs under the sign of death, for her mother dies while in labor.

Woe is me!
She died the hour that I was born.
I have heard the gray-haired friar tell
How on her death-bed she did say,
That she should hear the castle-bell
Strike twelve upon my wedding-day. (ll.196-201)

This hour is indeed an odd one not just by virtue of the mother's death, but in light of Leoline's own absence. Although the narrative claims that the following morning "he rose and found his lady dead" (l.335) thus suggesting a degree of surprise, the presence of the gray-haired friar negates this aspect of the unforeseen. The latter's presence at the hour of Christabel's birth evidences the knowledge that her emergence into the world will visit immediate death upon her mother, preventing her from visually recognizing and accepting that Christabel has indeed become a separate entity. Prior to this sudden separation, the mother has only known union with her child. Existence within the womb blocks the mother's realization of the child as an other. Its survival becomes completely conditional upon the well-being and desires of the mother, and it is here that maternal power is first established and exerted. The child develops and gestates within a constant state of subjugation during which time the mother retains control over its life. It is this power that the mother desires to recuperate after the birth of the child. Its inevitable loss finds expression in childbirth, the moment in which the child asserts itself as independent other. The pain of this break is echoed in the cries of both mother and child, but that maternal power which had previously articulated itself in the nurturance of the child within the womb is recaptured by the refusal to acknowledge the child's identity as a separate being. The immediate death of Christabel's mother preserves the intensity of a bond established by the pregnancy; she is abruptly prevented from gradually recognizing and accepting this new development. Her desire to linger even in death is expressed by her wish to be present on her daughter's wedding day. The mother's departure seems to be contingent upon witnessing her daughter's marriage to another, and yet the articulation of her desire seems to bind the two only closer, creating an enclosed system of existence that precludes the presence of anyone else. Within this system, it becomes impossible for Christabel to develop palpable relationships with the men who belong in her life. The very absence of her lover, whose welfare remains questionable and uncertain, speaks to the mother's refusal to relinquish her daughter to another. He who would vanquish the mother becomes vanquished himself, and by extension so too does Leoline since he would also be the means by which a marriage would be arranged. Once married, there would be no justification for the mother to remain. Within the mother's power, Christabel remains in a state of innocence which preserves not only her status as daughter/child, but also the mother's own as sole maternal figure. The sexual awakening that attends the wedding night is the same by which the possibility of pregnancy for Christabel becomes introduced.

The "Conclusion to Part I" signifies a change in Christabel's status as innocent and uncontaminated. Having "sinn'd" (l.381) the night before, she becomes an object of interest for the narrator.

> It was a lovely sight to see
> The lady Christabel, when she
> Was praying at the old oak tree.
> Amid the jaggéd shadows
> Of mossy leafless boughs,
> Kneeling in the moonlight,
> To make her gentle vows;
> Her slender palms together prest,
> Heaving sometimes on her breast;
> Her face resigned to bliss or bale—
> Her face, oh call it fair not pale,
> And both blue eyes more bright than clear,
> Each about to have a tear. (ll.279-91)

Christabel, after her union with Geraldine, is re-cast as an erotic object whose appeal seemingly resides in the sorrow and pain that characterize her loveliness.

This description of her praying in the forest is related in a manner designed to recreate a moment of fascination with a newly sullied object. Her beauty, previously associated with her spiritual state, takes on a more sensual air, and she becomes vulnerable to an eye that cannot help but revel in her fallen condition. That previously inhabited state of existence seems to have precluded the narrator from articulating a worldly depiction of her and his ability to do so now only testifies to her deliverance from the womb. As much as she may have been barred from seeing others (by their absence), so too have they been barred from seeing her. The sudden detailed physical description of her heaving chest, sighs, tears,[8] and facial expression speak to the immediacy of her presence as well as an accessibility to her person. Her re-birth out into the world is a contaminated one which mocks its own previous state of spiritual purity as emphasized by her prayerful posture that elicits a sensual description.

The narrator's characterization of Christabel "with open eyes (ah, woe is me!) / Asleep, and dreaming fearfully" (ll.292-3) and the present tense usage of the verb, re-casts the first part of the poem as a dream rooted in actual events, thereby explaining the quality of their movement as steps "that strove to be, and were not, fast" (l.113), as well as the deep sleep that afflicts the animals in the forest. Inasmuch as the mother must be made to recognize her child as a separate entity, so must the child—Christabel is, therefore, compelled via her dream to witness her own expulsion from the womb, the importance of which is emphasized by her open-eyed sleep.[9] As she does so, Geraldine adopts a maternal posture, thus re-creating the moment when mother and child are poised to visually recognize one another: "And lo! the worker of these harms, / That holds the maiden in her arms, / Seems to slumber still and mild, / As a mother with her child" (ll.298-301). Geraldine may appropriate the role of the mother but her deformed breast offers no nourishment, thus situating her as a perverse mother, one who rather than feeding her child, feeds *off* of her for her own personal revitalization. The passivity that attends Christabel's behavior is also marked by a connotation of having been birthed.

> Her limbs relax, her countenance
> Grows sad and soft; the smooth thin lids
> Close o'er her eyes; and tears she sheds—
> Large tears that leave the lashes bright!
> And oft the while she seems to smile
> As infants at a sudden light! (ll.313-8)

Not only is Christabel likened to an infant, the characterization of her smile alludes to the visual experience of a newborn in the first moments of life whose inability to see clearly necessitates that her reaction be informed by light—the sudden presence of which attends her emergence from the darkness of the womb. This "new beginning" for Christabel is marked by an awareness that dispels her transgressive propensities: "But this she knows, in joys and woes, / That saints will aid if men will call: / For the blue sky bends over all!" (ll.329-31). This reference to saints aiding men who call indicates an emerging awareness of a differentiation between the sexes, of the privileging of one over another. Despite her prayers, she knows she is forsaken on the basis of a divine preference for the male over the female. This realization, however, is followed by an immediate, but weak, negation that claims protection is all conclusive. She interprets the fact that this blue sky which "bends over all" (l.331) entitles everyone to divine aid as if it is blind to gender, and for the first time she acknowledges even if only subconsciously, her own inferiority.

Visual Infliction

Vision, which is the means by which Christabel is made to recognize her feminine status, is not simply that which is wielded by Geraldine in order to afflict others, it is a power to which she, herself, can be subjected. The inherent instability of vision[10] jeopardizes its bearer as easily as the one upon whom it is turned. For each instance in which she turns her eye upon Christabel, there is preceding that a moment of psychic torment, as if the potency of her eye can only manifest itself at the price of her own anguish. Christabel's trimming of the lamp casts the room in brightness and seems to render Geraldine weak. Although the angel lamp and religious icons may be said to subject her "evil" nature to pain, it is not the objects in and of themselves that weaken her, as much as it is her visual realization of them, for while the room is dark, she remains incognizant of any religious trappings about the room. It is only when the lamp is lit and she sees that it is fastened to an angel's feet that she immediately sinks down to the floor. The power of Geraldine's eye, with its punitive connotations that are first directed toward her and only later at Christabel, is, therefore, associative by nature. The images that appear to Christabel are not foreign to her and for that very reason have a displacing effect. Loaded with meaning and immediacy, these images function as a psychic blinding through which Christabel cannot navigate.

Christabel's complicity, however, becomes foregrounded in the moments leading to their union. Upon being told to disrobe by Geraldine, Christabel replies, "So let it be!" (l.235). By acquiescing, she relinquishes whatever right she may have had to any divine intervention above and beyond her mother's "appearance." Such a statement functions as her own directive to an unknown force signified by the invisible "you" which is understood as the subject of the sentence. She, therefore, places herself at its disposal. Although she tries to sleep, "vain it were her lids to close; / So half-way from the bed she rose, / And on her elbow did recline / To look at the lady Geraldine" (ll.241-4). Christabel is compelled to look upon Geraldine by her own eyes which refuse to close thus emphasizing a degree of curiosity as well as passivity. Her eye is drawn to that which she has never seen, re-situating Geraldine not as the one from whom orders flow, but to the more subservient status of one who is looked upon. She becomes the object of another's erotic interest as evidenced by Christabel's adoption of the posture of a lover waiting in bed. This then functions as an extension of the bride and groom scenario introduced by Christabel carrying Geraldine over the threshold. The mother's desire to be present upon her daughter's wedding day is also fulfilled by her invisible appearance which Geraldine detects and promptly dispatches. Geraldine, however, shows some reluctance.

> Beneath the lamp the lady bowed,
> And slowly rolled her eyes around;
> Then drawing in her breath aloud,
> Like one that shuddered, she unbound
> The cincture from beneath her breast:
> Her silken robe, and inner vest,
> Dropt to her feet, and full in view,
> Behold! her bosom, and half her side—
> A sight to dream of, not to tell!
> O shield her! shield sweet Christabel! (ll.245-54)

At the most voyeuristically pitched moment, the word fails. This sight to be dreamed of is not one accessible to the rational and wakeful mind and is, therefore, precluded by the logical rules that govern language. It is a moment when language itself becomes mortified, relegating the sheer horror of her mark to the realm of the subconscious thus implying that the true image of it can only be accessed through representation or allusion. The necessity of such an indirect approach speaks to an overwhelming potency the likes of which one cannot wholly experience without some degree of contamination. The very sight of the mark is not without an effect upon its bearer.

> Yet Geraldine nor speaks nor stirs;
> Ah! what a stricken look was hers!
> Deep from within she seems half-way
> To lift some weight with sick assay,
> And eyes the maid and seeks delay;
> Then suddenly as one defied
> Collects herself in scorn and pride,
> And lay down by the Maiden's side! (ll.255-62)

In her own moment of disrobing, Geraldine, in the full light of the lamp, not only reveals her physical affliction to Christabel, but is also faced with the confrontation of her own self which is defined by this indescribable deformity. Geraldine can no longer take refuge in the masquerade, the tales she creates, or in a fictive persona. This is also a moment when the human body as mask fails since it only serves to emphasize this deformity/mark of her true identity as something inhuman, as that which does not belong in this world. The body as mask, as shroud even, since Geraldine is in a state of temporary decay, fails to cover her completely and in so doing accentuates what should have remained unseen. She cannot conceal herself, her "old" and "cold" bosom (ll.457-8), within this mask of skin.[11] The hesitation which she seems to exhibit toward Christabel, therefore, has a double origin. It stems from a reluctance to expel Christabel from her enforced "sanctuary" of innocence made possible by Christabel's own charitable and well-intentioned behavior; it is also, however, rooted in Geraldine's own recognition of herself as an object of repulsion, the power of which can only be unleashed by its exposure to another.

The agony that appears to be caused by the sight of her own self is enough to compel her to look to Christabel for some intervening act. Her sudden defiance and seemingly unquestionable acceptance of the mysterious imperative is a sadeian reaction to the realization that Christabel's inaction signifies an unwillingness to help or save herself. This non-desire for self-protection functions as an invitation to harm. Geraldine, subjected to Christabel's gaze, recognizes in the latter a desire to know the nature of her deformity, the full effect of which can only be experienced through the immediacy of touch.

Once Geraldine's "mark of shame" (l.270) is shared with Christabel, it leaves an indelible vision that cannot be shaken even in the light of day. As she observes Leoline's fondness for Geraldine, Christabel suddenly recalls the "the vision of fear, the touch and pain!" (l.453) thus re-introducing the events of the previous night. This revelation and the disclosure of Geraldine's serpentine eyes become accessible only through Christabel's recollection, since the very narrative of the poem seems to have fallen under the same spell of silence cast upon her. This is also an instance in which Christabel's fear testifies to her acquisition of knowledge since she is able to recognize that the embrace offered by her father expresses fondness but sexual interest as well—it is after all this very act which elicits in Christabel that image of Geraldine's "old" and "cold" breast (ll.457-8). Her recollection of this particular aspect betrays the true context of Leoline's affections. This recognition prompts her to interfere, the consequence of which is the turning of Geraldine's eye upon her.

> The maid, alas! her thoughts are gone,
> She nothing sees—no sight but one!
> The maid, devoid of guile and sin,
> I know not how, in fearful wise,
> So deeply had she drunken in
> That look, those shrunken serpent eyes,
> That all her features were resigned
> To this sole image in her mind:
> And passively did imitate
> That look of dull and treacherous hate! (ll.597-606)

Geraldine's spell which bars Christabel from speaking the truth confines language to the dictates of the eye, but the means by which it does so are insidious. In Christabel's case, the image presents itself to her, in turn eliciting a desire to reveal the truth which then activates the suppressive function of the spell that doesn't completely silence her voice as much as it re-translates her intention. The image of Leoline embracing Geraldine provokes Christabel to action since prior to this scene, there is no indication of her desire to reveal what transpired the night before. The passivity which attends the "feminized" Christabel is used to the advantage of the gaze that seeks to proactively appropriate the power of the word by placing language in double jeopardy. The desire to speak becomes the means by which the word and its linguistic import will fail. Barred the dignity of silence, language for Christabel will only signify that which it does not mean. Rather than having the capacity to reveal the truth, she can only express an unlikely and cryptic hope: "All will yet be well!" (l.472).[12]

Until her union with Geraldine who also exhibits a degree of lack, Christabel has only known other people through their absence. Her lack of experience with physical and visual immediacy compromises her and leaves her vulnerable to an onslaught of images which seem designed to psychologically overwhelm her. Christabel's characterization as one having "deeply . . . drunken in" (l.601) juxtaposes the voracity of her gaze with the passivity of her eye which can only function as a lens through which the images pass and imprint themselves upon a disordered mind. Geraldine's look askance carries within it a deluge of truth about her real nature/identity that renders Christabel a vessel through whose eyes visions have been instilled.[13] These reshape her entire being, making her physical body vulnerable to a compromised mental state without the mediating force of consciousness.[14] The sight of Geraldine in the embrace of the Baron and the sheer brightness of the daylight prevent Christabel from taking refuge in the darkness that accompanied her existence within the womb. There is no recourse for her own eyes but to absorb what is before her in an all too visually clear world, an act that further relegates her to the helpless role of a spectator.

The Exclusion of Language

The spell which Geraldine casts upon Christabel is designed not only to prevent her from revealing the impropriety of their sexual liaison, but also to preserve Geraldine's masquerade, which proves that her expulsion of Christabel from the womb is the means by which another objective is to be accomplished. "'In the touch of this bosom there worketh a spell, / Which is lord of thy utterance, Christabel! / Thou knowest to-night, and wilt know to-morrow / This mark of my shame, this seal of my sorrow'" (ll.267-70). Knowledge is characterized by permanence. What Christabel will come to know that evening is not that which can be discarded; instead, it is that which will remain and culminate in the recasting of Christabel as a reflection of Geraldine's afflicted state. The immediacy of touch in the intimacy which Geraldine fosters becomes contaminatory. The sexual nature of her approach is a necessary one since Christabel's initiation would render her impure and, therefore, unfit to remain within the womb which can only sustain that which remains uncontaminated.[15] The inherent sterility of the environment with its connotation of innocence cannot withstand her sexual maturity. The injunction which bars her utterance, emphasized by the narrator's own interjection ("A sight to dream of, not to tell!" l.253), and the ensuing silence which settles over the narrative suggest the very act of Christabel's passage from the womb out into the world, an experience which can only elude language.

Inasmuch as Christabel may be compelled to see more clearly, so too is she made to be seen. With her expulsion from the womb, Christabel ceases to be the object of her mother's proprietary gaze, one to which she herself has been blinded by the consummate darkness of her environment. That gaze, however, bestows privilege upon its object as one from whom all others are barred. Christabel, despite her lack of awareness, is a figure around whom all things center. Once removed from the womb, however, she is relegated to the lesser role of spectator—one whose sole function it is to watch and whose passivity guarantees his/her non-intervention. Christabel's efforts to speak are thus attempts not only to reveal the truth, but also to reject the spectatorial position she has been made to occupy. As such, Geraldine's stultifying glances respond to Christabel's rejection of her new status.

Christabel's uncontrollable reactions testify to her newly acquired visibility as evidenced by the father's inability to ignore her odd behavior. Her request, "By my mother's soul do I entreat / That thou this woman send away!" (l.616-7) evokes from the narrative added information about the mother: "For her, and thee, and for no other, / She prayed the moment ere she died: / Prayed that the babe for whom she died, / Might prove her dear lord's joy and pride! / That prayer her deadly pangs beguiled" (ll.628-32). It is the mother's death bed prayer which binds Christabel and Leoline together in a mutually exclusive relationship based on devotion to no one but each other. Such a state makes no provision for progress without which life remains suspended and non-productive. The mother's prayer and proprietary desire undermine Leoline's patriarchal power (as evidenced by his chronic sickness and forgotten shield) by robbing him of the ability to commodify his own daughter by giving her to another man. It is a system of exchange to which the mother will not consent, and a precedent that if allowed to proliferate, would jeopardize the need to propagate. With the mother devoured and Christabel expelled, her visual accessibility invites her objectification, heightened by her monstrous behavior (which by extension carries the connotation of a thing rather than a person), by way of Geraldine and Leoline's respective looks.

Christabel's invocation of her mother elicits a rage from the Baron that precludes him from even speaking to Christabel, the consequence of which is her disappearance from his own linguistic system: "And turning from his own sweet maid, / The agéd knight, Sir Leoline, / Led forth the lady Geraldine! (ll.653-5). The degree of disregard for Christabel that the Baron shows is emphasized by the act of physically turning away from her.[16] In so doing, Christabel is vanquished from his scopic field and replaced with Geraldine whom he leads away. In rejecting his own daughter, so too does he sever the tie to his wife in favor of the possibility of renewing a friendship[17] and acquiring a new wife. The ability to "discard" Christabel, the act of which emphasizes her new status as an object, leaves her vulnerable to the likelihood of being given to another man, of being integrated into a system of exchange.[18] Geraldine thus makes the re-establishment of the masculine/patriarchal power possible, a necessary act since the feminine, in its articulation through the maternal, seeks to possess and hold close that which "belongs" to it, thereby promoting an all too exclusive existence with little hope for propagation. Left to herself, Christabel's existence becomes nullified by the absence of everyone else's gaze.

"The Conclusion to Part II" further emphasizes Christabel's disappearance by referencing an anonymous father and child. In a poem, for which she is named, she becomes textually expelled and wholly insignificant. Rather than the conclusion even indirectly addressing her, it instead concerns itself primarily with the figure of the father and an ambiguously gendered child (the likes of which Christabel once was), thus, testifying to the restoration of the patriarchal in the poem. The final lines function as an odd and cryptic elaboration for the source of Leoline's rage, the awkwardness of which reflects his own frenzied emotional response.

> A little child, a limber elf,
> Singing, dancing to itself,
> A fairy thing with red round cheeks,
> That always finds, and never seeks,
> Makes such a vision to the sight
> As fills a father's eyes with light;
> And pleasures flow in so thick and fast
> Upon his heart, that he at last
> Must needs express his love's excess
> With words of unmeant bitterness.
> Perhaps 'tis pretty to force together
> Thoughts so all unlike each other;
> To mutter and mock a broken charm,
> To dally with wrong that does no harm.
> Perhaps 'tis tender too and pretty
> At each wild word to feel within
> A sweet recoil of love and pity.
> And what, if in a world of sin
> (O sorrow and shame should this be true!)
> Such giddiness of heart and brain
> Comes seldom save from rage and pain,
> So talks as it's most used to do. (ll.556-77)

There seems, in this characterization of the father and child relationship, a sadistic impulse which is wrought by a father's inability to fully express the depth of his affection for his child. That an excess of love can only be expressed in bitterness, that rage and pain articulate themselves through "giddiness," that there is at least some degree of pleasure to be gained from uttering hurtful words convey the sentiment of this conclusion in frightening terms: paternal love can only realize itself in the infliction of pain upon its child. The love of a father can never find its adequate expression in language, the frustration from which rearticulates itself in gestures indicative of its opposite. The failure and inadequacy of language invites harmful behavior as if its function is that of mediation, to provide the father with some recourse other than to harm his child. The sheer intensity of the emotion, however, makes this an impossible endeavor. Unable to absorb and contain the feeling, as Christabel is forced to do, the father must transfer them unto the child whom he will discard as a consequence if necessary. Unlike the maternal that seeks an all too exclusive possession of the child, the paternal too easily discards him/her. This, however, is only alluded to by the poem, the extent of which is not even present in the conclusion, for the concluding lines end with what Coleridge cannot bring himself to say in the permanence of the written word.

Notes

1. Herb Galewitz, ed., *Mother: A Book of Quotations* (Mineola, NY: Dover Publications, Inc., 2002), 40.

2. Samuel Taylor Coleridge, "Christabel," in *English Romantic Writers*, 2nd ed., ed. David Perkins (New York: Harcourt Brace, 1995), 529-537.

3. The pupil expands and widens when one sees something which is pleasing or desirable. In keeping with this notion the pupil also contracts when one sees the opposite, that which is repulsive or undesirable. Desmond Morris' *The Human Sexes: Languages of the Sexes*, dir. Dan McCabe and Bob Burns, TLC, 1997.

4. Jane Gallop, "The Immoral Teachers," *Yale French Studies* 63 (1982): 124.

5. According to Julia Kristeva, "Freedom with respect to the maternal territory then becomes the pedestal upon which love of God is erected" (162). The Virgin Mother in being the means by which Christ is revealed to mankind is consequently elevated to her own religious status. "We live in a civilization where the consecrated (religious or secular) representation of femininity is absorbed by motherhood. If, however, one looks at it more closely, this motherhood is the fantasy that is nurtured by the adult, man or woman, of a lost territory; what is more, it involves less an idealized archaic mother than the idealization of the relationship that binds us to her, one that cannot be localized—an idealization of primary narcissism" (161). Julia Kristeva, *The Kristeva Reader*, ed. Toril Moi (New York: Columbia University Press, 1986).

6. As in Jonas Spatz's view in "The Mystery of Eros: Sexual Initiation in Coleridge's 'Christabel,'" *PMLA* 90:1 (Jan. 1975): 112.

7. Diane Hoeveler contends that the tenuousness of Christabel's identity stems from the idea that "she is a woman defined by herself and her creator in relation to men." Diane Hoeveler, *Romantic Androgyny: The Women Within* (University Park: The Pennsylvania State University Press, 1990), 179.

8. The tear as characterizing the eye with a particular attractiveness is mentioned as early as 150 A.D. in a passage from Achilles Tatius' *Leucippe and Clitophon*. The tear is

believed to confer a "peculiar loveliness" upon a "sweet" eye as well as a degree of eroticism with a touch of sadism: "When such an eye grows moist with tears, it is like the swelling nipple of water in a bubbling spring . . . tears held swimming in the eye seem to smile." Achilles Tatius also meditates on the act of looking/vision as invested with malevolent forces, as in the "evil eye," as well as a physical sexual power: "Such outpouring of beauty flowing down through [the eyes] into the soul is a kind of copulation at a distance. This is not far removed from the intercourse of bodies—it is in fact a novel form of intimate embrace" (Achilles Tatius, 183).

9. Coleridge's "inspiration" for a figure such as Geraldine is often traced to a dream he claims to have had: "I was followed up & down by a frightful pale woman, who I thought, wanted to kiss me, & had the property of giving a shameful Disease by breathing in the face / & again I dreamt that a figure of a woman of gigantic Height, dim & indefinite & smokelike appeared—& that I was forced to run up toward it—& then it changed to a stool—& then appeared again in another place—& again I went up in great fright—and it changed to some other common thing—yet I felt no surprise." Samuel Taylor Coleridge, *The Notebooks of Samuel Taylor Coleridge*, ed. Kathleen Coburn, 2 vols. (New York: 1957; 1961); entry 848, entry 1250. This account is also cited by Hoeveler and in A.H. Nethercot, *The Road to Tryermaine: A Study of the History, Background, and Purposes of Coleridge's "Christabel"* (Chicago: University of Chicago Press, 1939).

10. The Greeks tended to privilege visual perception over the other senses, although the sophists were concerned with the capacity of appearances to be false. Since then, there has been an ongoing debate about the power, nature, and trustworthiness of vision. Augustine debated the value of intellectual over physical vision with whom the medieval theologians agreed, thus privileging the invisible over the visible and introducing the "antiocularist" movement which was more appropriately characterized as antisensual. During the Renaissance, vision gained more credibility due to the importance of the printed word. For in-depth discussions of these issues, see Simon Goldhill's "Refracting Classical Vision: Changing Cultures of Viewing" and Janet Soskice's "Sight and Vision in Medieval Christian Thought" in *Vision in Context: Historical and Contemporary Perspectives on Sight*, ed. Teresa Brennan and Martin Jay (New York: Routledge, 1996).

11. For a discussion on Geraldine as a representation and mirror of Coleridge's castration fears at the hands of his mother, see Hoeveler, 169-175.

12. See Karen Swann's "Christabel and the Enigma of Form" for a discussion on Christabel's inability "to tell" as a result of hysteria. *Studies in Romanticism* 23 (Winter 1984): 533-553.

13. Geraldine's look is also Jean Starobinski's regard which Norman Bryson characterizes as a repetitious act that "indicates an impatient pressure within vision, a persevering drive which looks outward with mistrust and actively seeks to confine what is always on the point of escaping or slipping out of bounds. The regard attempts to extract the enduring form from fleeting process . . . it tend[s] toward a certain violence (penetrating, piercing, fixing), and its overall purpose seems to be the discovery of a second (re-) surface standing behind the first." Norman Bryson, *Vision and Painting* (New Haven: Yale University Press, 1983), 93.

14. This idea is reminiscent of the fifth-century sophist, Democritus, whose materialist optics were based on the notion that the eye was capable of receiving eidola, or "little images," from an object. Simon Goldhill, "Refracting Classical Vision: Changing Cultures of Viewing," in *Vision in Context: Historical and Contemporary Perspectives on Sight*, ed. Teresa Brennan and Martin Jay (New York: Routledge, 1996), 15-28. The

idea of a physical ray connecting the viewer and viewed bestows a degree of intimacy as well as passivity.

15. Spatz discusses Coleridge's views on love and sex as well as Christabel's own "attempt to come to terms with her sexuality" by projecting her fantasies onto Geraldine (111).

16. Wendy Stallard Flory takes an optimistic view in "Fathers and Daughters: Coleridge and 'Christabel,'" *Women and Literature* 3:1 (Spring 1975): 5-15. "Although her father turns from her, and Geraldine is 'lord of her utterance' . . . the power that these two have over her is only superficial—her moral integrity and sense of personal identity remain intact and inviolable" (11). Flory contends that since Christabel does not bear the physical deformity that Geraldine does, the harm done to her is relatively impermanent.

17. As in the view of Jane Nelson in "Entelechy and Structure in 'Christabel,'" *Studies in Romanticism* 19 (Fall 1980): 375-393. Her article also focuses on the relevance of Christabel's name as evoking the recognition of their opposites: Christ/Satan, Abel/Cain.

18. Goldhill's essay relates an account in which Socrates contends that the very act of looking can engage one in an economics of exchange that emphasizes the feminine body as a hunting net that lures the gaze of men. He notes that a particularly attractive Greek woman, Theodote, relies upon her admirers for her livelihood, men whom she allows to view her beauty (21). Within this context, Leoline's turning away from Christabel in favor of Geraldine further emphasizes her fall from grace and beauty, both of which have been conferred upon Geraldine by his act of leading her away.

Chapter Three

To Spare a Fly and Harm a Son: Hitchcock's Norma Bates

> Hush now baby don't you cry / Mama's gonna make all of your / Nightmares come true / Mama's gonna put all of her fears into you / Mama's gonna keep you right here / Under her wing / Hush now baby, baby don't you cry / Mama's gonna check out all your girlfriends for you / Mama won't let anyone dirty get through / Mama's gonna wait up til you come in / Mama will always find out where / You've been
>
> —*Pink Floyd,* "Mother"[1]

Hitchcock's *Psycho* is a film in which the power of the seen and the unseen manifest themselves in different registers. Sight signifies the extent to which one can fail to recognize the self as an object vulnerable to the desires of others by an overriding need for introspection, the look inward, as in the case of Marion. For Mother, however, with her empty ocular cavities, what was once available to her as sight becomes transformed into an all-encompassing and possessive gaze directed upon Norman. As relevant as the figure of the eye may be, however, language, itself, is equally foregrounded in the struggle that attends Mrs. Bates' desire for possession of her son. The potency of the gaze and its superiority to vision are played out in the physical murders of Marion and Arbogast, but Norman's own psychological demise can only be wrought by a silencing of his own voice made possible by Mother's transferential declaration, "I'm Norma Bates!" The utterance of this disembodied voice makes Norman's absorption into Mother's scopic field inevitable and permanent.

The Unseen Seen

The discomfort elicited by Marion's open eye is rooted in more than just the knowledge of her desire to rectify her wrong-doing or in having witnessed her murder. Her open eye which fills the frame is, instead, a commentary on her failures. The money which so compulsively attracts her gaze while she packs her suitcase appears to be the means by which Sam's financial responsibilities will be relieved which in turn would allow him to marry her. Thus, her desire for their relationship to be legitimized is ironically the impetus for the theft. Unable to see properly when she had actual physical sight (which in her case is articulated as an inability to recognize what lies beneath the surface), she now meaninglessly "sees" all. Death for her is the infliction of blind sight, of vision robbed of the capacity to recognize. The extreme clarity of Marion's eye sees everything and everyone as nothing; it is the reassignment of the living to object status that elicits feelings of fear and insignificance.[2] However much Marion's eye may be indicative of her punishment, it is also an assault upon the living, for they are confronted with a glimpse into the void which is more terrifying than the void itself. It is in this instance that the condition of death becomes less fearful than the realization that we are already inhabited by death which is merely masquerading behind signs of life.

This revelation of an ever-lurking death becomes emphatically foregrounded by the eye's domination of the frame. The eye into which the shower drain dissolves implies a condition of waste that is detectable, an absence which can be seen in the eye. The lack of difference between the appearances of a living eye and a dead one indicates the cohabitation of death with life; the dead one in fact masks itself by appearing to see even more since the pupil becomes dilated. The pupil's own appearance as a hole, an absence, an orifice, is of course deceptive since the pupil does contain a jelly-like substance which is not particularly solid but tenuously present. It is a fragile existence: the eye, easily crushable, reflects the security of one's identity. That one cannot differentiate the living eye from the dead one is also to say it is possible that there is little if any difference between life and death, that life shadows and is attendant upon death. This lack of a definitive boundary between life and death in an organ that provides an all too effective mimicry of the latter implies an intimate knowledge with it. Unbound in the eye of the dead, death becomes confrontational, demanding its own reflection in the eye of the living through a mesmerism which seeks to freeze not just the physical body but the movement of the eye itself, forcing one to stare, to mimic the look of the dead. In this moment of mimicry, the eye becomes an accomplice of death, the means by which the person to whom it "belongs" is controlled. It is as if the eye seeks what is disquieting and forbidden in order to be frozen, as if it is the only means by which it may gain a respite from the constancy of its own reflexively dictated movements.

Our feelings of insignificance and absence from our own selves wrought by the confrontation with death also compromise the supposed security that accompanies one's sense of self or subjectivity. If one's subjectivity is largely constituted by visual perception which in itself can be illusory, then the self, rather than resting on a firm foundation, is actually situated upon a lack, a lurking emptiness that one seeks to deny. The refusal to recognize this contributes to the shock of seeing Marion's empty gaze—as Norman so adeptly deflected her discomfort into introspection, so too does Marion's eye function as deflection: rather than one's fear remaining focused upon the character in the movie, it turns inward for the sake of revelation.[3]

But the death of the eye is also the freedom of the gaze, for without the constricting limitations of the eye and the body, it is now able to absorb all that is before it. The ability to gaze, to see so expansively, is a freedom which mocks the very limits of the physical body and is at the root of the seemingly conflicted relationship between the eye and its beholder. The inability to control the eye's very movements and its tendency to pursue the forbidden are motivated by a gaze which seeks mastery over the body in a final bid to rid itself of an encumbering and constricting mass. The death of the eye is the means by which one is able to transcend his limited subjectivity and merge with the gaze of the world, thus allowing one to gaze upon others, subjecting them to their own lack, to their own void within.

The inferiority of physical sight to the gaze is one of the main concerns of the film. The manner in which both victims, Marion and Arbogast, are killed emphasizes this notion, for although they are last seen with their eyes open, their ability to see fails to prepare them for the ensuing attacks. Confronted by the gaze that seeks possession of an object through its death, vision as seen in these characters is either unable to meet the gaze and must constantly avert itself, or it shocks itself into inaction. Within the world of *Psycho*, Norman's eyes are the means by which Mother's gaze pulls focus, that his eyes are discernable during the attack in the shower, characterizes the eye as not only capable of the harmlessness which attends the reflective quality of a mirror, but can also be subject to a mirror's singular depth—indifferent and dismissive of Marion and Arbogast's struggles. The eye that Marion seems to have almost smugly attracted in the person of Norman is an eye which will expose her to death at the "hands" of Mrs. Bates.

The Reiterated Image

Part of the intricacy of *Psycho* remains in the different registers that reflection itself occupies. There are reflections which are disregarded while others are recognized, as well as those which precede the objects to which they belong. It is this latter aspect, however, that finds its correlation in language which in its articulation calls events into being. What is said or is heard being thought becomes disastrously literalized, as if language dissatisfied with its intangibility seeks its own translation in concrete terms; in other words, it seeks its own reflection. This is strikingly apropos for a world in which Mother's existence is given credence via voice, for she, herself, is a disembodied spirit who seeks permanent possession of her son. Like language, she cannot be confined, remaining, instead, omnipresent and all transgressive. Her presence is, therefore, detectable before Marion arrives at the Bates Motel—Mother is actually present in the voice of Sam, Marion's boyfriend.

Marion's suggestion that Sam come for dinner to her home where her mother's picture can confer respectability upon their relationship and her sister can join them, elicits the following reply from him: SAM, *picks up his shirt and sits in a chair*. "And after the steak, do we send Sister to the movies . . . turn Mama's picture to the wall?"[4] His response is uncannily similar to Mother's angry retort to Norman's explanation for feeding Marion: WOMAN. "And then what, after supper? Music? Whispers?" The correlation of one response to the other lies not only in the grammatical structuring of the questions and the number of suppositions posed, but also in the alluded-to parallelisms of Marion's sister, Lila, working in the Music Makers Music Store, and the turning away of Mother's picture in order for Marion and Sam's "improper" behavior not to be seen functions as the visual equivalent to the whispers Mother fears will be exchanged. To avert Marion's mother's eyes is the same as whispering to Mother since both are attempts to deceive each one's primary mode of knowing. It becomes apparent that Marion is destined for Mother who seems to temporarily have possessed Sam linguistically and in gesture, for his sitting in the chair anticipates the posture in which Mrs. Bates has been mummified and will eventually be revealed. The arm of the chair in which Sam sits, however, casts a glint of light juxtaposing his agreement to see Marion "respectably" with the light that will later be cast by the peephole in which Norman will watch her disrobe: SAM. "All right. Marion, whenever it's possible, I want to see you. And under any circumstances—even respectability." Sam's willingness to comply with Marion's desire for legitimacy heightens the later impropriety of Norman's behavior. Sam's use of the word "see" invokes the context of dating, of developing a meaningful relationship. For Norman, however, seeing can only be defined in its literal sense since he is barred/incapable of achieving this other context of "seeing" by his own mother. "Respectability" is a condition that will never be known to Norman or Marion.

It is a sense of shrinkage, fatedness, and enclosure which permeates the movie to the extent that reflections and images not only operate as foreshadowings, but also convey the feeling of limitation, as if there is a very small pool of resources and choices from which to draw. After Marion returns to the office, Cassidy arrives with the forty thousand dollars intended to purchase a home for his daughter and new son-in-law. The painting of a lake above Cassidy's head remains visible as he speaks of the impending marriage while that of a dessert looms over Marion. Both paintings signify the consequences of the choice which Marion must later make. For her to remain with Sam is to engage in a fruitless relationship. For her to take Cassidy's money is to disappear in another body of water, that of a swamp. Both pictures allude to pre-destined points.

It would be comforting to have the option to believe that these characters have the freedom necessary to truly make choices, but the claustrophobia and sense of entrapment is expressed in Sam's frustration: SAM. "I'm tired of sweating for people who aren't there. I sweat to pay off my father's debts, and he's in his grave. I sweat to pay my ex-wife alimony and she's—living on the other side of the world somewhere!" The absent have what seem to be an inescapable hold upon the living. Death and living on the other side of the world (which alludes to a more peripheral existence) do not guarantee another's freedom. Sam is fettered by financial constraints, debt that remains as abstract as the people for whom they have been incurred. Norman's constraints, however, in his all too literal world are signified by the motel, the establishment of which was made possible by his mother's money but becomes a debt, by forcing Norman to maintain it.[5] Rather, than Norman drawing the causal connection between his mother and the motel, it is Sam who unconsciously verbalizes the link: SAM. "You look frightened. Have I been saying something frightening?" NORMAN. "I don't know what you've been saying." SAM. "I've been talking about your mother, about your motel. How are you going to do it?" Sam's words not only emphasize the link, but also establish yet another reflection of Mother whose presence has already been literalized by her corpse. With only a pause between "about your mother, about your motel" both objects become equivalent to one another. The vacancy of the motel becomes indicative of Mother's own lack of vital signs.

The policeman who wakes Marion in her car functions as another arm of Mother. Not only do the sunglasses which completely conceal his eyes find their echo in Mother's empty ocular spaces, but his unfinished advice further paves the way to the Bates Motel: OFFICER. "You slept here all night?" MARION. "Yes. As I said, I couldn't keep my eyes open." OFFICER. "There are plenty of motels in this area. You should've—I mean, just to be safe." It is as if Mother, aware of Marion's preference to sleep in her car rather than in a motel, compels the officer to take action. The long arm of the law becomes Mother's appendage, and the officer's advice, appropriately absent in its completion, compels Marion to act upon what had never been said.

Having given her advice, the officer follows her until he veers off toward the town of Gorman. Although it may appear that there are two possible destinations, that of Gorman and Norman, the overwhelming similarity in name is enough to insinuate that encounters with Norman, however likely, are still avoidable. Such a notion becomes compromised by the fact that the officer spies Marion a short time later in the midst of trading in her car—it is as if the roads on which Marion travels interconnect and lead only to one destination: the Bates Motel.

The growing limitations upon her freedom are, therefore, not only wrought by the guilt of having stolen the money, but by the law and the very landscape. Her involvement with Sam, who is often characterized as a more masculine version of Norman, and her flirtation and possible attraction to Norman indicate a world that is shrinking around Marion, forcing her toward a particular destination. Her very progression from Sam to Norman illustrates a literal lessening in stature until she encounters Mother who is the slightest in physique yet the most deadly.

Language Lost: Repetition and Disruption

Although Marion's physical appearance situates her as a double for Norman, she is also linked by a linguistically based frustration.[6] While discussing her unhappiness with the status of her relationship with Sam, she gropes for more appropriate words to express herself.

> MARION. Oh, Sam, this is the last time.
> SAM. Yeah? For what?
> MARION. For this. For meeting you in secret, so—we can be secretive. You come down here on business trips, and we steal lunch hours. I wish you wouldn't even come.
> SAM. All right. Marion, whenever it's possible, I want to see you. And under any circumstances, even respectability.
> MARION. You make respectability sound disrespectful.

Like Norman, Marion is forced into reiteration, moments when the word itself becomes its own definition. In the company of Sam, she experiences this "loss" for words as if the very impropriety of their erotically charged relationship precludes her from attempting to invest it with any meaningful linguistic legitimacy. The wish to fully convey the reasons for her dissatisfaction as a bid to propel Sam toward more acceptable behavior is never realized. Without that adequate articulation, Sam's acquiescence also lacks depth and understanding as evidenced by the sudden emergence of his financial frustrations. He comes to truly comprehend and accept her conditions only after it is too late, writing his letter to her after she has already been murdered as an indirect consequence of having stolen the money which she believed to be Sam's only impediment to marrying her.

As much as repetition may be the consequence of an inability to articulate the depth of her (erotic) frustration, it can also indicate a stark realization as evidenced by the exchange with Cassidy.

> CASSIDY, *ignoring him*. Do you know what I do about unhappiness? I buy it off. Are uh—are you unhappy?
> MARION. Uh, not inordinately.
> CASSIDY. I'm buying this house for my baby's wedding present. Forty thousand dollars cash. Now that's—that's not buying happiness. That's just buying off unhappiness.

As Marion leaves the office, Caroline stops her: CAROLINE. "Aren't you going to take the pills? They'll knock that headache out." MARION. "Can't buy off unhappiness with pills. I guess I'll go put this money in the bank then go home and sleep it off." Rather than ingesting the pills offered by Caroline, Marion ingests Cassidy's belief. Her use of the phrase "buying off unhappiness" signifies the integration of that particular idea not only into her vocabulary, but also into her psyche. The utterance functions as a conversion during which Marion suddenly accepts and eventually adheres to the tenet expressed by Cassidy.

Repetition for Norman, however void of meaning it may appear to be, is significant for the different levels on which it operates. His reiterative compulsion suggests that he is linguistically confined which is another aspect of that sense of entrapment he weakly attempts to deny. It also, however, functions as a safety mechanism that prevents him from having to think for himself which is one of Mother's primary duties (NORMAN. "No, uh—well, I run the office, and uh, tend the cabins and grounds, and—and do little errands for my mother—the ones she allows I might be capable of doing"), as well as a characterization of Mother, herself, as one who has made a return. Norman becomes caught in a linguistic loop that further characterizes the volatile exclusivity of his and Mother's relationship.

> OLD WOMAN'S VOICE. *No! I tell you no!* I won't have you bringing strange young girls in here for supper! By candlelight, I suppose, in the *cheap, erotic* fashion of young men with *cheap, erotic* minds!
> NORMAN'S VOICE. Mother, please!
> OLD WOMAN'S VOICE. And then what, after supper? Music? Whispers?
> NORMAN'S VOICE. *Mother, she's just a stranger!* She's hungry and it's raining out.
> OLD WOMAN'S VOICE. "*Mother, she's just a stranger.*" As if men don't desire strangers. Oh! *I refuse to speak of disgusting things, because they disgust me!* Do you understand, *boy*? Go on! Go tell her she'll not be appeasing her ugly appetite with my food, or my son! Or do I have to tell her 'cause *you don't have the guts?* Huh, *boy*? *You have the guts, boy*?
> NORMAN'S VOICE. *Shut up! Shut up!* (emphasis mine)

In this short exchange that Marion overhears from her motel room, not only do Mother and Norman repeat their own words, but Mother also mockingly mimics him. Repetition becomes the means by which Norman is linguistically trapped, but in an odd twist also becomes the signifier of his intermittent control over Mother. When Mother repeats herself as she does in this exchange, Norman remains tenuously dominant over her. Although his denigration is the overriding concern of the conversation and indicative of his Mother's hold over him, it is still he who "puts the words in her mouth." As linguistically limited as Norman may be, at this point Mother is even more so. To hear Mother's voice riddled with repetition is to know that Norman still exists.

Norman's "control" over Mother is linguistically and physically exerted in their second exchange.

> NORMAN. *Now, Mother*, um—I'm gonna bring something up . . .
> MOTHER, *laughs*. I am sorry, *boy*, but you do manage to look ludicrous when you give me orders.
> NORMAN. *Please, Mother.*
> MOTHER. No! I will not hide in the *fruit* cellar. Ha! You think I'm *fruity*, huh? I'm staying right here. This is my room and no one will drag me out of it, least of all my big, bold son!
> NORMAN. They'll come *now, Mother*. He *came after* the girl, and *now* someone will *come after* him! *Mother, please*, It's *just for a few days. Just for a few days* so they won't find you.
> MOTHER, *mocking*. *"Just for a few days?"* In that dark, dank *fruit* cellar! No! You hid me there once, *boy*, and you won't do it again, not ever again! *Now get out! I told you to get out, boy.*

> NORMAN. I'll carry you, *Mother*.
> MOTHER. *Norman*! What do you think you're doing? *Don't* you touch me! *Don't*! *Norman*! *Put me down! Put me down!* I can walk on my own. (emphasis mine)

This is a moment in which Norman most dominantly asserts himself, for his pleas in the first exchange which were clearly dismissed by Mother, become unyielding ones in the second with which Mother has no choice but to conform. Despite the rampant repetition, words are expressed in variations: fruit/fruity, came after/come after. However slight the differences may be, they are still navigations through different forms and tenses of the words, thus indicating a degree of self-assurance. Norman's linguistic assertiveness is also supported by repetition but, this time, of an act as identified by Mother ("You hid me there once, boy, and you won't do it again"). Having hidden her once before, he becomes empowered and predisposed to doing it again.

The apparently iterative nature of Norman's linguistic structure prevents him from digressing. His exchange with Marion when she first arrives at the motel is the same as the one he will later offer to Arbogast.

> MARION. Do you have a vacancy?
> NORMAN (to MARION). Oh, we have twelve vacancies.
> NORMAN (to ARBOGAST). I'm always forgetting to turn the sign on, but we do have a vacancy. Twelve, in fact. Twelve cabins, twelve vacancies.
> NORMAN (to MARION). Twelve cabins, twelve vacancies. They, uh—they moved away the highway.
> NORMAN (to ARBOGAST). See, that used to be the main highway right there.

With the realization, however, that Arbogast is looking for Marion, Norman's only recourse is to re-frame the same dialogue within a negative context in the hope that Arbogast will leave.

> NORMAN (to MARION). But...there's no sense dwelling on our losses. We just keep on lighting the lights and following the formalities.
> NORMAN (to ARBOGAST). Well, I'll tell you the truth, I didn't really forget to turn the sign on. It just—just doesn't seem like any use anymore, you know?
> NORMAN (to ARBOGAST). Well, I'll tell you, I don't even much bother with guests registering anymore. You know, one by one you drop the formalities. I shouldn't even bother changing the sheets, but—old habits die hard. Which reminds me— (*He flicks a wall switch. The sign: "BATES MOTEL—VACANCY" lights up outside.*)

Because Marion is so similar to Norman, he is able to converse with her despite some initial stuttering rooted in nervousness due to his attraction to her. Arbogast, however, is completely unpredictable and resists the linguistic appropriation (signified by his constant interruptions) that Marion unwittingly acquiesces to and results in her death. He is, therefore, allowed the opportunity to leave, an option that he refuses and pays for with his life.

For Norman, repetition is a means of preventing disruption, disruption which Marion never realizes has been caused by her arrival. The audience remains largely unaware as well, but is offered a glimpse into its nature only after Marion has been killed. When Lila walks into the hardware store looking for Sam, an older woman is seen and heard discussing insecticides and the necessity of painless death for both insect and man. The woman's matronly appearance and preoccupation with death establishes a link to Mother who was just "seen" stabbing Marion; her expression of disapproval in a fleeting assessment of Lila further associates her with Mother's own reaction to Marion. This disapproval may stem from jealousy or even resentment since Lila interrupts a dialogue between the older woman and the young male attendant. The importance that the woman places on her opinions fails to be reflected in the attendant's response who seems, instead, to regard her statements as prattle. The arrival of Lila ends their discussion and the woman wordlessly, with the exception of a "thank you," leaves after making her purchase.

Lila's appearance and its effects are a sanitized and non-lethal version of her sister's own arrival at the motel. The dialogue in which Norman and Mother had engaged in for years in this place/area that had been forgotten once the highway was moved, was not only interrupted but also threatened: the attention that Norman paid to his mother was diverted to Marion. Having heard the heated exchange between Norman and Mother regarding her and her "ugly appetite," an exchange which evidenced an unstable woman, Marion, perhaps over-estimating Norman's regard for her, the basis of which is his attraction to her, makes the suggestion that contributes to her fate: to put Mother away. Because of the odd circumstances which attend Mother's presence, to put her away demands that she be consigned to the grave, thus, silencing her dialogue with Norman.

The Reflection and Its Rejection

Prior to her intrusion upon Mother and Norman, Marion must first make the choice that will pave her way toward the Bates Motel. While she packs her suitcase, she is often compelled to look at the money laying on her bed as if vacillating between stealing it or not. As she moves about the room, pictures of a child, presumably her, and a couple who seems to be her parents, are visible behind her. As incognizant as she is of these pictures, she is also of her own reflection in the mirror. It is no surprise that the frame in which she is shown "looking" at herself portrays a more complete image of Marion within the boundaries of the mirror, than it does outside of it. The "real" Marion with her back to the camera, and, thus, even more fragmented than her reflection, can only be recognized within the mirror. Her facial expression, accessible only by way of her reflection, lacks familiarity with her own image, and instead registers distance indicating the extent of her introspection. It is as if the sudden look inward bars her from recognizing herself as someone still honest and criminally untainted. This particular frame in the movie is divided in half, with her reflection to the left, and Marion, herself to the right, thus, illustrating the division within her while also dramatizing her turn away from the mirror. This turning toward the money is a visual rejection of who she once was, as signified by her abandoned reflection as well as by the pictures from her past. Having done so, she places the money in her purse and leaves with her suitcase.

While Norman shows Marion into the office to register, their reflections become momentarily conjoined within a mirror by the sign-in desk. Although they are strangers to one another, the reflection implicates them as aspects of one another.[7] The similarity of their physical appearances does not become obvious until their reflection is torn apart, and they stand face to face on opposite sides of the desk. In its sheer intangibility, that reflection which only seems to be wrought by chance, testifies to the invisible power of Mother and the fatedness of Marion's arrival.

Marion, having overheard Norman and Mother's argument, meets him outside her door: MARION. "I've caused you some trouble." NORMAN. "No. Uh—Mother—m—my mother, uh—What is the phrase?—She isn't quite herself today." Norman's reply coincides with the appearance of his reflection, but it is a reflection that precedes him. Norman, who appears to be his own person, is instead led by another. Inaccessible to Marion from her point of view, the reflection signifies what will always escape Marion—in this peripheral world away from which the highway has been moved, the intangible other, epitomized by Mother's hold over Norman, is given primacy and as such cannot be guarded against or even be detected.

During their discussion in the parlor, Marion's genuine desire to help Norman cope with Mother elicits an admission from him which emphasizes the unique role that language plays in his and Mother's relationship.

> NORMAN. People never run away from anything. The rain didn't last long, did it? You know what I think? I think that we're all in our private traps, clamped in them, and none of us can ever get out. We scratch and—and claw, but only at the air, only at each other. And for all of it, we never budge an inch.
> MARION. Sometimes we deliberately step into those traps.
> NORMAN. I was born in mine. I don't mind it anymore.
> MARION. Oh, but you should. You should mind it.
> NORMAN. *Oh, I do, but I say I don't.*
> MARION. You know, if anyone ever talked to me the way I heard—the way she spoke to you—
> NORMAN. *Sometimes when she talks to me like that, I feel I'd like to go up there—and curse her—and—and—and leave her forever! Or at least defy her.* But I know I can't. She's ill. (emphasis mine)

Norman alludes to his use of language as a means of denial that in this particular instance pertains to his feelings about being trapped and confined by Mother's demands upon him. In a larger context, however, it is the denial of Mother's death that compels him to initiate conversations with her corpse—language then becomes the means by which death is kept at bay. To unsuspecting Marion and the audience, hearing "Mother's" voice is indisputable evidence of her existence in more conventional terms, for the assumption is made that for every audible voice, there must be a living body to which it is attached.[8] But Mother does become a burden to Norman and his only recourse is to wish he could attack her verbally. Having poisoned her when she was alive only to mummify[9] her later, Norman unwittingly renders her immune to any further physical violence. His desire to curse and leave her, followed by the alternative of defying her, exposes his preference for a more verbal attack. Unfortunately, Norman knows such an attack would compromise, what seems to him, Mother's already fragile existence—to defy her is to dare her to speak for herself, to find her own voice, the failure of which would necessarily mean her death; or Norman would feel compelled to provide her with his own voice, thus, resulting in his defying himself. Killing Mother again or baiting himself into his own attack are not viable options. The realization that he cannot correlates with his movement from one of leaning forward to that of leaning back. Having done so, the frame becomes overrun with doubles: two pictures in opposition as well as two stuffed birds posed in attack formation. Norman's "counterpart," however, is a shadow of another stuffed bird which is perched upon a branch—this shadow then speaks of an as of yet unknown threat that Norman's mental state poses, the capacity of the un-palpable to do physical harm, and the faceless image of Mother that appears in the shower scene. The act of sitting back then becomes the signifier of Norman's acquiescence to the double life demanded by Mother.

Norman's lack of complete control over Mother is evidenced by her intrusion upon his and Marion's discussion. This "appearance," however, is visually undercut by the concealment of her presence in the physical source of her utterance: Norman. Marion's suggestion to commit Mother is met with deep-seated hostility.

> MARION. Wouldn't it be better if you *put her . . . someplace*?
> NORMAN. You mean an institution? A *madhouse*! People always call a *madhouse "someplace," don't they. "Put her in—someplace."*
> MARION. I'm sorry. I didn't mean it to sound *uncaring*.
> NORMAN. What do you know about *caring*? Have you ever seen the inside of one of those places? The laughing and the tears . . . and the cruel eyes studying you. My mother there? But she's *harmless*! Wh—she's as *harmless* as one of those stuffed birds!
> MARION. I am sorry. I only felt—It seems she's hurting you. *I meant well.*
> NORMAN. *People always mean well.* They cluck their thick tongues and shake their heads and suggest, oh, so very delicately. Of course, I've suggested it myself. But I hate to even think about it. She needs me. It—it's not as if she were a—a maniac, a raving thing. *She just goes a little mad sometimes. We all go a little mad sometimes.* Haven't you?

MARION. Sometimes just one time can be enough. Thank you.
NORMAN. Thank you, "Norman."
MARION. Norman. (emphasis mine)

Conspicuously absent from Norman's statements is repetition wrought by frustration or an inability to find more appropriate words; here, repetition has a double function, that of emphasizing the unacceptable and as a mode of deflection. The biting eloquence and inflection may be communicated in Norman's voice, which is only the surface, but they are more indicative of someone other than Norman, namely, Mother. The strength of her outrage at the thought of her own institutionalization is enough to not only compel Norman to speak *her* mind, but to also infect his own natural speech patterns. Nor can Norman control his own physical movements (an aspect that comes to have more lethal consequences). His act of leaning forward, which accompanies the rebuke, serves not only to physically emphasize *her* anger, but to also frame him within the context of a game bird. On the mantle behind Norman's head, sits a stuffed pheasant against which Mother's physical control over Norman can be measured. When Norman leans forward in anger, his head obscures the pheasant's in such a way that its body appears to be an extension of his head—this position indicates the possession of Norman's mind. In the act of sitting back, his head obscures the pheasant's body, implying that Mother has relaxed her hold upon him, and that Norman, like the body of the bird is destined to be stuffed by Mother in order to achieve permanent possession of her son.

By posing the question, "We all go a little mad sometimes. Haven't you?" Norman places the responsibility of a verbal reply upon her, one which causes her to assess her situation before answering. Her discomfort becomes assuaged by this re-direction of her gaze, which is already pre-disposed to introspection, toward a garnering of some insight about herself. That predilection for looking within rather than without results in her vision being relegated to her own self. Rather than utilizing it as the primary mode of knowing others, she instead relies upon her auricular capabilities to form opinions about others. Her mistaken conclusions about the depth of Norman's unhappiness with Mother based upon a single overheard conversation proves that judgments informed by her hearing are inaccurate. This, of course, leaves her particularly vulnerable to Norman and Mother whose verbal exchanges are rooted in fiction. When she does see outwardly, that is, at Norman in the parlor, she manages to detect his threatening character. Although discomforted by his mannerisms and anger, a more gentle tone of voice coupled with a question eliciting the realization that stealing the money was her own little act of madness dismisses any fears Marion may have had.

Norman's addendum to Marion's expression of thanks (NORMAN. "Thank you, 'Norman'") seems to be a fairly innocuous one, but certainly has signification. In a more benign situation, Marion's use of his name would emphasize her gratitude and also function as recognition of a degree of intimacy formed by his having helped her realize the gravity of her mistake. Here, however, his wish articulates the struggle of Mother's re-emergence. Having relaxed her hold over Norman, she again asserts herself but not without some difficulty. Norman's correction is marked by maternal inflection, the type that every child has heard as a lesson in properly expressing one's gratitude. Mother, who had orchestrated Marion's chastisement, desires to be thanked for the wisdom of her words, but Norman's frustration with feeling trapped by Mother's demands articulates itself through his desire for the invocation of his name, the utterance of which would momentarily allow him the freedom and separation from Mother that he can only crave but never fully realize. Fortunately for Mother, she, too, gains by Marion's agreement to repeat Norman's name, for the nature of that maternal correction has the capacity to seemingly transpose Marion's own identity with that of Norman as a child. Rather than remaining his double, one who is similar in appearance and circumstance, she becomes an actual surrogate for him. "Thank you, 'Norman'" also functions as a direct address from Mother to Marion whom the former has chosen to re-name as her son. Marion's unwitting acquiescence to her new identity is expressed by abiding to the addendum.

Due to Marion's introspective predilection, she remains unable to perceive herself as others do, that is, as an object of an other's gaze. The failure to recognize her own image is the failure to recognize her own potential for objectification, that is, as a passive *thing* to be possessed or even discarded. That she is incognizant of Norman spying upon her, that she does not feel like she is being watched, speaks to this very problem.

The peephole, appropriately hidden by a picture of a woman being ravished, is of course another representation of an eye. The jagged edges which frame the hole itself are remarkable similar to the edges of Mother's own ocular spaces. Furthermore, the peephole functions as the realization of Norman's own desperation which he had articulated earlier ("I think that we're all in our private traps, clamped in them, and none of us can ever get out. We scratch and—and claw, but only at the air, only at each other")—the jaggedness and direction of the edges, themselves, are suggestive of that same clawing and scratching initiated from within the parlor. Norman's failure to derive any satisfaction from having watched her is a moment in which he too realizes that, like Marion, he must also resolve to break free of his own personal trap known as Mother. The very parlor, as much as it may be his favorite and personal place, is still a microcosm of the house with its similar décor, that signifies Mother. As such, Norman cannot escape her mediating presence alluded to by the peephole which is tantamount to Mother's eye. As if believing that that a hole would somehow empower him and allow him access to a world free of her influence, he attempts to scratch his way out of the parlor, only to find that he himself in his effort to subject another to his gaze, can never elude that of Mother's. He uses this peephole as a means of attempting to "realize" some sexual desire that he is incapable of actually achieving. It is a desire that can only be whetted at a distance and like the white light, in its sheer intangibility which illuminates the hole, his desire can only be frustrated by this inadequate satisfaction of his appetite. The realization of his desires can only be substance-less as long as Mother remains.

Norman's own psychological fragmentation finds expression in this effort to separate from Mother. The wish to do so, to assert his own self, is wrought by a sudden emotional response to Marion, and, thus, lacks stability and strength. What becomes clear then is that Norman needs to be pushed if he is to have the chance of escaping Mother, yet the inability to follow through with conviction jeopardizes the impetus to do so, which in this case is Marion. Norman's incapacity to be his own person is evidenced by this, by the fact that his desire to separate from Mother is wrought by the desire to (sexually) join with another. This drive to co-mingle prevents him from ever experiencing wholeness of any kind which is certainly to Mother's advantage.

It is unfortunate that Marion deeply affects Norman, or as the psychiatrist will later say, "moves" him, for Mother does "allow" for the existence of the peephole and, thus, for Norman's attempt to satisfy a visual appetite. Because Marion entices him into thinking of leaving Mother, the very act of which is already an affront to her, it becomes obvious that Marion's appeal has progressed from a surface-oriented one to another of more resonance. Like the sweets that Norman constantly eats, which by their nature are empty food, lacking in nutritional value, Marion should have remained no more than "eye-candy," someone whose appearance is the sole source of value. To allow Norman any more would lead to a healthier physical and emotional development that would compromise both Mother's hold over him and her very existence. It is, therefore, imperative that Norman remain dependent, "un-whole" and "hollow," if Mother is to fully possess him later.

This sense of emptiness/absence within oneself is applicable to Norman, Mother, and the very world which they inhabit. The moving of the highway, which Norman laments to both Marion and Arbogast, designates this location to the periphery of the world, as if it had been deemed a destination that one should not venture toward. It can only be stumbled upon by those who "had gotten off the main road," the connotation being that this "hidden" location is reserved for those who have strayed or have rendered themselves unfit for society. This peripheral geographical existence compounds Norman's already lacking life which is marked by a deceased father and a murdered mother and her lover. This absence upon absence then becomes reflected in Norman's own psychological state that seeks to fill a lack with another void which is of course Mother and her corpse. Without anything of substance, this overwhelming sense of emptiness seems to take a physical toll upon the very landscape and the laws which govern it as if mirroring its only inhabitant. As Marion's blood mingles with the water in the tub, they flow down the drain in a counter-clockwise movement which further designates the location of the motel to the "other side" of the world since the "natural" movement of water is clockwise. The swamp also seems to be as deep as it is expansive since it is able to hide as many as four cars (Marion's, Arbogast's, and those of the two prior victims) at least two of which appear to be sunk one on top of another.

Time, itself, also appears to be affected by Norman and Mother's lifestyle. When Lila enters Mother's bedroom in search of her, her eyes are drawn to a bronze cast of a pair of hands. These "severed" hands which are "maternal" in appearance are grotesque not only in the disembodied solidity that they convey, but also in their lacquered appearance. The former functions as an appropriate characterization of Mother's corpse while the latter is juxtaposed with the roughly decayed texture of the body. Lila's fascination is broken by a look into the mirror above the hands and an initial misrecognition of her own reflection. Her fear, most likely heightened by the knowledge she is trespassing, may also stem from the realization that the fascination of her gaze with the hands rendered her vulnerable to the gaze of another without her awareness, thus, placing her in potential danger. As she turns to confront the reflection of her reflection, produced by the positioning of two mirrors that face one another, a time anomaly or lag becomes apparent,[10] for although Lila has already ceased to bend over the bronze cast and is now in an upright position, her reflection is still only in *the process* of doing so. Norman's effort to "reverse" time by bringing Mother back from the grave and his insistence upon preserving her, seems to have had a similar affect upon time itself, that of a slowing down.[11] This anomaly is followed by Lila noticing Mother's imprint in the bed, thus, Mother's existence becomes validated by an absence that testifies to her sheer physicality, to a heaviness that creates a deep impression in the bed.[12] And yet this absence is an all too literal representation of Mother as a body void of life.

The Shrinkage of Meaning

Psycho is a film in which particular words or turns of phrase are also arrested and rendered as undeviating in signification as the road to Norman on which Marion travels. Unfortunately the newspaper from which Marion takes her "cues" is a prime example of this tendency. While at California Charlie's car dealership,[13] she picks up a newspaper presumably to find out if there has been any report of the theft. After she folds the money inside this paper, and places it in her bag, the word, "OKAY" becomes obvious as part of the headline. The newspaper is next prominently featured while Marion is registering at the motel.

A newspaper is language whose meaning is not necessarily stabilized as much as it is left confined, immobilized, perhaps even mortified. By its nature, a newspaper reports only the facts, that which has indisputably occurred, and, therefore, precludes its reader from any interpretive act—the imaginative component that often attends the act of reading is blocked. Words take on singular meanings, as if the slippages that ordinarily attend and enrich language are eliminated. In a world such as Norman's that is already pre-determined by his routine and repetitious behavior, it is no surprise that Marion's response to her hometown being Los Angeles would have a particular implication. Unwilling to reveal the truth, she looks to the newspaper whose words, "Okay" and "Los Angeles" are visible as if the former word functions as assurance of the latter as a reply. But the words themselves are really only suitable for the context in which they are invoked within the paper. Marion mistakenly takes them out of context, applying them to a situation for which they are no longer applicable or have the capacity to render a different meaning to. The words themselves become hollowed out and divested of alternate meanings by their very appearance in the newspaper. Norman who was starting to reach for the key to cabin number three suddenly shifts toward and takes the key to number one as soon as Marion says, "Los Angeles." It is as if hearing the name of the city compels him to assign her to the other room without his even realizing the reason behind doing so.

Like Marion, for whom language can at times be unwieldy forcing her into the repetition of a word that becomes its own definition, Norman also exhibits a linguistic discomfort: NORMAN. "It—it might be, uh, nicer—and warmer in the office." MARION. "Well, it stopped raining." NORMAN. "Eating in an office is just—just too officious. I—I have the parlor back here." Marion, however, at least reverts to words whose meanings are applicable to what she is attempting to express. Norman, on the other hand, delegates meaning to the word according to a surface or auricular similarity; language, therefore, tends to be particularly volatile for him when strangers enter his world. Unlike Mother whose responses he can more or less predict and the repetitious nature of their verbal exchanges, strangers are wholly unpredictable and discomforting especially since their systems of linguistic signification are comparatively larger than Norman's. They, therefore, have to be drawn into a cycle of iteration as seen by Marion's repetition of Norman's name. By doing so she unknowingly acquiesces to a "role" as Mother's child, thus, allowing her to be lethally appropriated by Mother. Despite Norman's incorrect use of the word "officious" as a means of describing the atmosphere of the office, this excessive eagerness in offering unsolicited help becomes prophetically characteristic of his behavior in the parlor.

The newspaper's headline from which the word "Okay" has been prominently featured is fully revealed after Marion's death. While cleaning up Mother's "mess," he picks up the paper whose headline reads: "Voters Okay New Water District." Unbeknownst to Marion, she had been gathering assurance from a headline that all too literally defined the nature of her final destination: the swamp. The consignment of her body to this "water district" portrays language as a driving and determining force of which the characters are not aware, especially since Norman "fulfills" the sentiment of the headline without having even read the words themselves. It is as if any attempt to literalize the word, even for the sake of disseminating news, can only result in negative or dire consequences.

Marion's submersion is more than just disappearance, it's appropriation. She is integrated into the very landscape of Norman's world that becomes characterized by absorption and immersion due to the prevalence of water imagery, by being consigned to that unknowable other space which is the swamp, that dark void which finds expression in the patrolman's sunglasses, the drain, and her lifeless pupil. But all of these pale in comparison to the darkest void of all—the surprise that awaits Lila and the audience in the cellar.

Immediately following Marion's submersion, Sam is seen writing a letter to her.

> Saturday
>
> Dearest right-as-always Marion,
> I'm sitting in this tiny backroom which isn't big enough for both of us and suddenly it looks big enough for both of us. So what if we're poor and cramped and miserable at least we'd be happy. If you haven't come to your senses, and still

There is certainly an embeddedness of opposite sentiments expressed in this letter, the likes of which are not wholly dissimilar from Cassidy's view of happiness. For Sam, happiness can be found in being "poor and cramped and miserable" while for Cassidy happiness is not so much achieved as unhappiness is postponed. Although Sam certainly looks at the situation in a more positive light, there is still that tension caused by an inability to separate one extreme from another—the words themselves seem to breed their own opposites so that the causal connection of one word to another becomes questionable and unstable.

The unfinished letter also illustrates various registers of meaning undercut by the previous scene in which Marion is murdered. The interrupted line that reads, "If you haven't come to your senses, and still" would most likely have been completed with a sentiment expressing a committed acquiescence to her wish for respectability. *Roughly* paraphrased, Sam's retraction of his initial objections could presumably finish with "If you haven't come to the right decision [to leave me] and would still like to get married, then let's do it." His offer is predicated on the hope that she has not yet made the right decision which would be to leave him, and it is certainly a hope that has already been proven true—her desire to stay with him compels her to take the money showing the extent to which she has not "come to her senses." More ominous, however, is the literal translation of that particular phrase since Marion having been murdered is physically barred from "coming to her senses" ever again. Sam writes an all too literal characterization of Marion's current status without even realizing it—the layer of meaning which he is intent upon invoking functions as a screen that delays the revelation of the truth for him while emphasizing its brutality for the audience. Unlike Norman's world where language caught in a cycle of iteration can only, therefore, point forward to its already designated end, Sam's and everyone else's for that matter is a world where language tends to be bound by a delay, a look backward or even a lag, in which events and the act of realization attempt to catch up to words already uttered.

The Spectacle of Exchange

What would typically remain an abstract thought or desire finds its concrete, and therefore visual, expression in Norman and Mother's world. Marion's one instance of literalization demands her eventual death. As she drives further away from Phoenix toward Fairvale, she imagines Cassidy's reaction to her having stolen the money. CASSIDY'S VOICE. "Well, I ain't about to kiss off forty thousand dollars! I'll get it back, and if any of it's missing, I'll replace it with her fine, soft flesh! I'll track her, never you doubt it." What Marion so freely imagines is accepted as unquestionable fact by the audience. Her thoughts thus find their correlation in the nature of the newspaper and its unyielding context which only contributes to the lethal literalization of what she thinks will be Cassidy's reaction. The relish with which she enjoys the idea of having stolen his money can only be achieved by articulating the manner in which any missing money would be repaid. Although this is easily forgotten in the midst of her conversation with Norman and her ensuing decision to turn herself in, it is shortly afterward that the missing money becomes foregrounded once again. By taking a piece of paper and subtracting the money from the original forty thousand, she calls attention to the fact that there is, indeed, a sum of money that needs to be replaced; like the audience, however, she does not realize that she has already named the terms/conditions of repayment—flesh in exchange for money. The responsibility for the manner in which she is killed is highlighted by the frame where she expresses her desire to pull herself out of a trap before it's too late, and the frame where Mother appears with her upraised knife. The two are exact mirror reflections of one another, thus implying that it is Marion, herself, who has chosen death in the shower, when the flesh can be made "fine" and "soft."

Her stipulations for repayment also account for the manner in which the camera follows the movement of the knife, visually fragmenting her with each stabbing motion.[14] The fragmentation of Marion, of the body, testifies to the vulnerability and impossibility of wholeness for Marion, the likes of which would have been partially re-established by her return to Phoenix, and as said earlier for Norman. Because the idea of "wholeness" is a threat to Mother's existence, her attacks upon Marion's body are portrayed as particularly vicious as if the naked body for all its assertion of wholeness is simultaneously made to indict itself as vulnerable. The soft flesh which is easily torn testifies to the superiority of Mother whose own flesh in its rigor mortis state resists fragmentation and remains invulnerable.

Marion's death at the hands of Mother may be the repayment of her debt, but it is also a symbolic filicide. Given the similarities in Marion and Norman's physique, names, and circumstance, as well as Marion's "affirmative" response to her "re-naming" as Norman in the parlor, Mother may be interpreted as wreaking the physical death of a surrogate child. Despite his having poisoned her, Mother is barred from killing Norman by the need for his physical body.

She not only finds retribution through Marion's death but the desire, itself, to kill is the means by which she gains vitality. In the act of committing murder, Mother sheds the impalpability of a shade, that is, as one without physical consequence, and materializes as an inescapable entity. It is as if for each appearance or return, repayment must be made for her transgression into the world especially since hers is a return for which there should have been none. Once consigned to the grave, it became unnatural for her to have been removed, as if having experienced death results in her being barred not just from entering the realm of the living but also seeing them as well—her empty ocular cavities seem to irrevocably mark her immersion into death and contaminate the movie with other void-like imagery. The act of killing allows Mother to achieve union with Norman with each death resulting in an increased hold over him since he is forced to cover up her misdeeds. The need to do so re-establishes Norman's loyalty to Mother, thus binding them even tighter to one another.

Norman's effort to negotiate the void that is Mother manifests itself in his preoccupation with taxidermy, the nature of which also emphasizes the absences which characterize his physical and psychological life.[15] His statements and questions are riddled with references to his pastime.

> NORMAN. Boy, it's stuffy in here.
> NORMAN. It's all for you. I'm not hungry. Go ahead. You—you eat like a bird.
> NORMAN. My hobby is stuffing things. You know, taxidermy. And I guess I'd just rather stuff birds because I hate the look of beasts when they're stuffed. You know, foxes and chimps. Some people even stuff dogs and cats, but, oh, I can't do that. I think only birds look well stuffed because—well, because they're kind of passive to begin with.
> NORMAN. Well, it's—it's more than a hobby. A hobby's supposed to pass the time, not fill it.
> NORMAN. You've never had an empty moment in your entire life, have you?

This desire to take what was once living and re-animate it with sawdust and chemicals indicates a deeper lack in Norman's life which he attempts to fill with the concrete. The plethora of birds surrounding him in his parlor, however, speaks to the futility of his efforts. His predisposition toward literalizing is due to a limited imagination which is not only evidenced by the repetitious nature of his dialogues with Mother, but also by his need to "make a mental picturization" of Marion while answering Arbogast's questions. Although Norman feels the pressure to lie in order to protect Mother, his stuttering can only be alleviated with some admission of truth and his difficulty with "mental pictures" is exactly that. His unconscious need to literalize is also rooted in Mother's own desire for physicality which may explain his sudden decision[16] to place Marion in cabin one upon hearing that her supposed hometown is Los Angeles. While Marion stands in the parlor she is framed several times with the picture of an angel behind her. It is as if the very name of her hometown coupled with the angel in the picture invite Norman to frame Marion herself with the boundaries of the peephole. Marion's admission of her true name, "Crane," also marks her as a fairly passive bird, the likes of which Norman stuffs, further accentuating her object status. Mother, however, takes this even more literally by "stuffing" Marion with eight knife wounds and dispatching her to the afterlife.

When Norman sits in his chair and speaks to Marion, he becomes part of a concentric spectacle created by the illusion of the glassy-eyed stuffed birds, Mother sitting in the window of their house on the hill, and the audience watching the movie itself, all of which speak to Norman's wish to be seen/acknowledged which in this peripheral world can be difficult. The linguistic register in which Norman speaks, that of repetition, becomes akin to a script, thus creating an air of the theatrical, and providing Mother the cues with which to appear. Unfortunately the strangers who arrive are unaware that they have intruded upon an ongoing dialogue with a pre-determined ending—even Norman, himself, is not wholly cognizant since Mother temporarily expels him from his own body in order to commit her murders.

Mother, bereft of eyes, becomes the source from which the gaze emanates and its potency is seen in Norman's efforts to remain out of her direct line of "vision." As Marion attempts to anchor the gaze of her mother to her picture, so, too, does Norman disseminate Mother's to the various birds within the parlor. For Marion, her mother's gaze is powerful enough to dispel the impropriety that is at the heart of Marion and Sam's relationship—the ability to have dinner in front of her picture will legitimize their relationship. It is, however, essential that they have dinner in Marion's house not only because the home is a maternal space, but also because there is a limited area which falls within the gaze of the object, that being the picture. Once Marion anchors her mother's gaze, it remains potent, but it also becomes confined to a specific scopic field (the truth of which is articulated by Sam's suggestion that after dinner they turn her picture to the wall) and is, therefore, escapable. Norman, however, lives within a gaze that he attempts to filter through multiple objects, through which Mother's gaze can be mediated and a more tolerable visual field achieved. Although Norman, as a taxidermist, could insert glass eyes into Mother's ocular cavities, that would confine the gaze which would compromise the value of Norman's existence since he performs his duties for the sake of being "seen" by her.

There is no doubt that Norman is on some level aware of the potency of Mother's gaze, and he makes it a point to prevent his being caught in it unaware. By posing her in the window, he not only disperses her gaze, but also prevents himself from being caught in its exact line of vision when he walks into her bedroom since her back is to the door. The imprint on the bed also indicates that Mother is made to lie facing away from the door as well. When Norman carries her down the stairs to hide her in the basement, her line of vision does not encompass his own. It is Lila's interference, however, that signals Norman's psychic demise. When Lila encounters Mother in the basement, she touches her shoulder. In doing so, the corpse mysteriously swings away from the wall and toward the doorway. At the same moment, Norman enters with a knife and dressed as Mother. Given the angulation of Mother's head and the illusion of a rocking movement created by the swinging light bulb, once Norman steps down, he falls within her direct line of vision, a scopic field in which her gaze is concentrated. Norman who avoids looking in mirrors and noticing his reflection does so as a means of subconsciously denying the fact that all he is constituted by is solitude and his outward appearance which will later become Mother's own trappings.

With the prolonged disembodied scream of "I'm Norma Bates!" Sam appears from behind and wrestles the knife away. As they struggle, the dress is torn open in a manner that alludes to a cesarean section, and Norman, with a face contorted in agony, "gives birth" to Mother. The very embeddedness of Mother's name, Norma, within Norman's own, points to her inescapability. His chicken-like stature and compulsive Kandy Korn snacking (a play on the cornmeal fed to chickens) mark him out as one whose value resides in his consumption. She devours him as easily as she swallows the "n" at the end of his name, the very declaration impregnates Norman, permanently expels him from his own self, and leaves him a vessel for Mother to inhabit. Confronted with the sight of her own corpse, Mother in the guise of Norman takes refuge in him, since given the presence of witnesses, to return to it would be to vanquish herself to her appropriate resting place: the grave. Norman who filled his time stuffing dead birds, becomes a dead bird himself re-animated by Mother and given the appearance of life. In the final scene where Norman now Mother sits in the holding cell, the only movements s(he) makes are slight tilts of the head much like a bird and changes in facial expressions. Her disembodied voice, however, is heard.

> MOTHER'S VOICE: It's sad when a mother has to speak the words that condemn her own son, but I couldn't allow them to believe that I would commit murder. They'll put him away now, as I should have years ago. He was always bad, and in the end he intended to tell them I killed those girls and that man, as if I could do anything except just sit and stare, like one of his stuffed birds. They know I can't even move a finger, and I won't. I'll just sit here and be quiet, just in case they do suspect me. They're probably watching me. Well, let them. Let them see what kind of person I am. I'm not even going to swat that fly. I hope they are watching. They'll see. They'll see, and they'll know, and they'll say . . . "Why, she wouldn't even harm a fly."

Mother whose eloquence testifies to her presence repeats one telling phrase, "As if I could do anything except just sit and stare—like one of his stuffed birds" the same which Norman spoke to Marion in Mother's defense. By repeating this phrase, Mother's presence in the parlor becomes indisputable. Now that she has eyes, however, she becomes suddenly aware of being watched, of being the object of an unseen other's gaze.[17] Although one may argue that her repetition of the phrase from the parlor is actually a remainder of Norman, her gaze into the camera dispels that notion, for Norman, incapable of verbal defiance and a look into the mirror, would not be able to withstand the bold gesture of looking into the camera lens. Mother, however, having yet to see her "new" reflection seeks to replicate herself upon the audience's retinas while figuratively filling each with fear. Mother's gaze, originating in the void that is death, retains the power to mortify, but in this new body, gains the capacity to recognize and render visible her audience.

Notes

1. "Mother." By George Roger Waters. © 1979 Roger Waters Music Overseas Ltd. and Warner Chappell Artemis Music Ltd. All Rights Reserved. Used by Permission. Warner Bros. Publications U.S. Inc., Miami, Florida 33014.

2. The shock of the audience also evidences its complicity in her death. Kaja Silverman contends that "[a]t this point we find ourselves in the equally appalling position of the gaze which has negotiated Marion's murder, and the showing of the corners of the frame so as to simulate the perspective of a peephole insists that we acknowledge our own voyeuristic implication." Kaja Silverman, "The Subject of Semiotics," in *Film Theory and Criticism,* 5th ed., ed. Leo Braudy and Marshall Cohen (New York: Oxford University Press, 1999), 145.

3. The recognition of death via the open eyes of the deceased introduces another potentially frightening aspect. Since vision is linked to knowledge, the deceased appears to be perpetually witnessing his/her own demise, as if even in death there can be no rest. In the movie *Mercy* (2000), the murderess cuts the eyelids off of her victims in a symbolic attempt to prevent them (surrogates for her mother) from ignoring the sexual abuse inflicted by her stepfather. For the murderess, the eyelid symbolizes the ability to ignore what was obvious, to ignore her pleas for help and protection. The eyelid allows for ignorance, it also signifies indifference. The lowering of the lid is a disavowal of truth. The cutting away of it then assures knowledge and a forced realization of an ugly truth.4. Joseph Stefano, *Alfred Hitchcock's Psycho* (Universal City: Universal Home Video, 1998), DVD.

5. In "Links in a Chain," Leland Poague notes that money functions, not as a MacGuffin but as the "public fact" of the film, that which contaminates and informs every relationship in the movie. The building of the motel, financed by Mother at the behest of her lover testifies to her affection for another other than Norman. Leland Poague, "Links in a Chain," in *A Hitchcock Reader*, ed. Marshall Deutelbaum and Leland Poague (Ames: Iowa State University Press, 1986), 340-349. The motel also functions as the "offspring" of Mother and her lover's relationship. That Norman takes over its management may tie him to its constant maintenance, but it is also the means by which he "re-engenders" it, and thus re-casts himself in the place of his mother's lover.

6. Lesley Brill contends that Marion and Norman's lack of control over their own lives becomes reflected in their frustrations with language. "When the characters of *Psycho* speak, their sentences typically seem divided against themselves, at once trying to reveal and conceal the speaker." Lesley Brill, *The Hitchcock Romance* (Princeton: Princeton University Press, 1988), 232. Donald Spoto notes that this element of secrecy (although not apparent in a linguistic register) is also identifiable in the lives of the more minor characters: "wedding day tranquilizers taken by Janet Leigh's co-worker . . . ; the cash undeclared for taxes by the possessive father; the bottle of whiskey hidden in an

employer's desk; the secrets of illicit affairs . . . and undiscovered murders." Donald Spoto, *The Dark Side of Genius: The Life of Alfred Hitchcock* (New York: DeCapo Press, 1983), 421.

7. As in William Rothman's view. William Rothman, *Hitchcock—The Murderous Gaze* (London: Harvard University Press, 1982), 267.

8. The disembodied voice and the desire to see the body to whom it belongs is explored by Michel Chion in his essay, "The Impossible Embodiment," in *Everything You Always Wanted to Know About Lacan (But Were Afraid to Ask Hitchcock)*, ed. Slavoj Zizek (London: Verso, 1992), 195-205.

9. In "Psychosis, Neurosis, Perversion," Raymond Bellour contends that "the omnipotence of infantile desire turned towards death" can be signified by a play on "Mommy" and "mummy" in which "the mother's body, fetishized to death, so to speak, becomes the body that murders, in keeping with the desire awakened in the eye of the subject possessed by it." Raymond Bellour, "Psychosis, Neurosis, Perversion," in *A Hitchcock Reader*, ed. Marshall Deutelbaum and Leland Poague (Ames: Iowa State University Press, 1986), 324.

10. Many thanks to my husband and colleague, Anthony Miccoli, for drawing my attention to this "hiccup" in time.

11. As in David Sterritt's view: "The atmosphere of both bedrooms [Mother's and Norman's] is that of a secret world where stasis and retention—paralysis—have always been the rule, rather than movement or transformation." David Sterritt, *The Films of Alfred Hitchcock* (New York: Cambridge University Press, 1993), 112. Norman's own method of taxidermy ("needles and thread, sawdust") is more indicative of a process employed in the 1800's by upholsterers who sewed up animal skins and stuffed them with rags. This method was abandoned in the early twentieth century in favor of more artistic approaches evolving into the preservation and placement of the animal skin upon a model of its body.

12. Rothman reads Lila's recognition of herself within Mother's mirror as a moment in which Lila's startling reflection becomes the means by which Mother is made momentarily alive and present (322).

13. See Poague's "Links in a Chain" (344), for a discussion on the cultural relevance of cars and their license plates in the movie.

14. See Edward Recchia's "Through a Shower Curtain Darkly: Reflexivity as a Dramatic Component of *Psycho*" in *Literature Film Quarterly* 19:4 (1991): 258-267 for a discussion on Hitchcock's use of the camera as a means of establishing the audience's identification (also noted in Rothman) and separation from Marion in the shower scene—forcing us into sharing her horror one moment, but maintaining our observer status the next. Hitchcock's constant re-directing of the audience's identification also occurs in the peephole scene in which we are aligned with Norman's own point of view only to be shifted into the position of a spectator twice removed from the action of film. For another discussion on viewer identification and the revelation of a split in their desires between "squeamishness and curiosity," see Spoto, 422-425.

15. Brill notes that Norman's taxidermy is also the transformation of his deep childish fondness for stuffed animals which remain in his bedroom, thus attesting to his arrested development (229). Mother's mummification is a stark departure from the comfort offered by stuffed animals with their softness, warmth, and pliability, which only increase with time.

16. This sudden change of mind is interpreted by Rothman as an act of hesitation characterizing the camera's ambivalence about its own nature which demands that

Marion's fate be sealed upon having been singled out by the camera's eye. The camera is also a mother's gaze which gives birth to Marion's world once it passes through the open window, but simultaneously penetrates a world already in existence, the act of which betrays its masculinity. Camera is both mother and son foreshadowing the imbricated identities of Mother and Norman. For this and more insightful remarks on the camera's role in *Psycho*, see Rothman, 245-341.

17. Rothman also suggests that the person being seen is not Mother but Norman situating himself as an actor/speaker/author of a monologue—"a silent spectator within the theater of his own consciousness" (337).

Chapter Four

Breaking the Bond: Eugenie's Triumph in the Bedroom

I'm a mother, / And I take like a mother / I understand blood / And I understand pain / There can be no life without it never doubt it / I'm a mother / I'm a vessel of life / I got the trauma here to prove it
—*The Pretenders,* "I'm a Mother"[1]

As in many of de Sade's works, *Philosophy in the Bedroom* features a maligned and cruelly "abused" character, one whom the libertines consider so ideologically loathsome that an orgy of defilement is orchestrated in her honor. This event, however, also marks the re-birth of another character: Eugenie. In violating and mutilating her own mother, she annihilates her point of origin, the one in whom she was conceived and the site from which she emerged. In doing so, Eugenie destroys the gaze of the maternal by not only rejecting the supposed rights her mother claims to have over her, but also by desecrating the very bond and body that dictates the behavior of a child toward its mother. Eugenie triumphs over a mother whose attempt to reclaim her daughter results in the emergence of a libertine prodigy who so gleefully proclaims, "Here I am: at one stroke incestuous, adulteress, sodomite, and all that in a girl who only lost her maidenhead today!" (359).[2]

Such a statement hearkens back to the sexual initiation of Christabel and Norman's "devotion" to his mother. Eugenie, however, is no Christabel whose own virtue is the tool by which her mother confines her. In the unquestionable sexual innuendo that characterizes her night with Geraldine, Christabel's loss of innocence cannot be tolerated by the womb-like environment that demands darkness[3] and sterility. Eugenie on the other hand is guided by Madame de Saint-Ange's command: "Fuck, Eugenie, fuck, my angel; your body is your own, yours alone; in all the world there is but yourself who has the right to enjoy it as you see fit" (221).[4] Nor is Eugenie Norman whose words betray his weakness and lack of conviction resulting in his possession by his mother.

The aspect that links Eugenie most to Pentheus, however, is located in an issue of consciousness, a sadeian pursuit. Unlike Pentheus, Eugenie achieves a heightened sense of self-awareness, that even the frenzied momentum of an orgy cannot diminish. The violation elicits from Eugenie a realization of the many ways she is perceived in relation to her mother in the singular moment of a stroke. The degree to which such consciousness escapes Pentheus is emphasized by the discarding of his dress and wig, a move that insinuates recognition as surface oriented, and by the sheer impenetrability of Agave's "blindness" that reframes him as an animal to be hunted.

The Purpose-full Mother

In attempting to retrieve Eugenie, Madame de Mistival seeks to re-confine Eugenie within a visual space that has been compromised by the latter's departure. Her removal from the home, that space sacred and often synonymous with the mother, signifies a blindness/ignorance regarding the activities in which Eugenie may be involved. Madame's objection to Eugenie's traveling alone, that is, without eyes upon Eugenie to guard her behavior, causes Madame de Mistival to "imagine all sorts of things" (350) according to her husband's letter. However accurate these imaginings or visions of fancy may be, she insists upon remedying them by returning Eugenie home since to do so would restore the child to her own power. Eugenie, however, has entered the home of an anti-mother and a return home is no longer a demand to be made, but a request whose fulfillment is conditional upon Eugenie's willingness to do so. Madame de Mistival unfortunately labors under the delusion that as a daughter Eugenie will not break or desecrate the bond (rendered fictitious by the teachings of Dolmance) between mother and child, that she will instead readily acquiesce to the beckoning of her mother.

Madame de Mistival's arrival at the home of Madame de Saint-Ange and subsequent demand for the return of Eugenie is not met with the compliance which the former seemingly expects. Confronted by the state of undress that she finds in Madame de Saint-Ange's home, Madame de Mistival's concern centers around Eugenie's physical rather than psychological person. She fails to consider the possibility of her daughter's psychic development, that which has revealed Eugenie to be a libertine at heart, because it is that which would mark the latter as her own person completely dissimilar from her mother. Mortified by what has obviously transpired, Madame remains concerned with the care and education that she has invested in Eugenie, and only afterward does she fear for Eugenie's soul. That refusal to recognize and to accept what Eugenie has always been will certainly cost her.

Incorrect in assuming that the etiquette that dominates the world from which she comes also operates within the walls of this house, she asserts herself as a woman toward whom respect ought to be shown. She fails to realize that the governing code is more similar to the one with which she is intimately familiar, the one that condones her husband's ill use of her and allows him to request of Madame de Saint-Ange that Eugenie be "instructed." The concluding line, "I am most content to leave the first gatherings to your hands, but be well convinced however that you will have labored in some sort in my behalf" (350) serves as an overriding affirmation of the lessons taught to Eugenie and assertion of his rights to his daughter over those of the mother.[5] Although physically absent from the text, Monsieur de Mistival's wishes lurk in the background and overtake those of his wife's.[6] What she is most unprepared for, however, is the response she receives from Eugenie herself. Upon commanding Eugenie to depart with her, Madame de Mistival is met with a refusal that elicits the latter's disbelief and provides the libertines with "just cause" to abuse her.

In the mind of Madame de Mistival the fact that she is mother to Eugenie establishes her rights and ownership to her daughter. This is evidenced not only by the commands she gives Eugenie but also by the offense she takes at being denied. In this sadeian world, however, motherhood itself is a veritable abomination raised to sanctification by the fallacious tenets of Christian religion. It is not she who reveals the truth of maternal instinct, but interestingly enough, Madame Saint-Ange:

> MADAME DE SAINT-ANGE. Dread not infanticide; the crime is imaginary: *we are always mistress of what we carry in our womb*, and we do no more harm in destroying this kind of matter than in evacuating another, by medicines, when we feel the need. (emphasis mine)
> EUGENIE. But if the child is near the hour of its birth?
> MADAME DE SAINT-ANGE. Were it in the world, we should still have the right to destroy it. In all the world there is no prerogative more secure than that of mothers over their children. No race has failed to recognize this truth: 'tis founded in reason, consecrated in principle. (249)

If these sentiments seem remotely familiar it is because Saint-Ange articulates the very principles that compel the behaviors of characters such as Mrs. Bates, Agave, and even Christabel's deceased mother. So frightening are the implications, however, that they can only be voiced by a female character easily abhorred for her "immoral" conduct and who subscribes to a code wherein men profess preferences for "sodomy, sacrilegious fancies, and penchants to cruelty" (247) and women must be "implacable enemies to wearisome child-getting" (248), opting for abortion whenever possible. In Saint-Ange, one finds that embracing perversity allows for an honesty and truth that Agave and Mrs. Bates actively deny yet covertly pursue and of which Madame de Mistival remains entirely incognizant. Interestingly enough, however, it is also Madame Saint-Ange who contends that a child in being her offspring is also *owed* a share of her wealth "rightfully the child's by virtue of the same intimate alliance" (224). This idea is a revolutionary one when compared to the maternal figures thus far, for only she speaks in a language of indebtedness, albeit monetarily, to the child. In doing so, Madame de Saint-Ange counters the often invoked contention that it is the child who is situated in a position of obligatory gratitude. The specification of *monetary* indebtedness in its simplicity, and thus possibility of payment that would erase the debt, is juxtaposed with the complexity that characterizes the emotional debt demanded by the mother upon the child; the expectation of repayment is alluded to and invoked by the mother, but never truly desired and thus can never be repaid. This illusion of indebtedness to the mother is explored and exposed as a lie by Dolmance.

As Angela Carter notes, "[The Mother] is the perpetually violated passive principle; her autonomy has been sufficiently eroded by the presence within her of the embryo she brought to term. Her unthinking ability to reproduce, which is her pride, is, since it is beyond choice, not a specific virtue of her own" (124). Thus the false pride and hypocrisy that de Sade's libertines so vehemently rail against begins to become apparent.

> MADAME DE MISTIVAL. What! My daughter is to disobey me and I am not to be able to make her sensible of the rights I have over her!
> DOLMANCE. And what, if you please, are these rights, Madame? Do you flatter yourself they are legitimate? When Monsieur de Mistival, or whoever it was, spurted into your vagina the several drops of fuck that brought Eugenie into being, did you then, in the act, have her in mind? Eh? I dare say you did not. (353)

The brutality with which Dolmance speaks implicates de Sade himself as the character's double for the question of having thought of the child, him or herself, in the midst of intercourse is one that plagued the writer. A lack of intent toward the existence of the child introduces an element of randomness and mere chance which can arguably undercut any duty owed to a mother or father, particularly since it is de Sade's contention that the behavior, care, or obligation toward children is dictated by the society within which they are raised. Madame de Mistival's "rights" are thus invalid and the bond between mother and child which she believes Eugenie will recognize is dismissed. By justifying her claims to Eugenie on the basis of her status as mother she is also evoking the libertine contention that motherhood perpetuates in children the illusion of duty, while affirming as virtuous that maternal attitude of passivity most evident in the wording of her request to Madame de Saint-Ange ("I beg you, Madame, to be so very good as to return her to me, and not to disapprove my request or behavior" [352]). Although the mother may appear to be victimized by her child, the manner of response toward that victimization is deemed appropriate to that particular role and, therefore, what she is most admired for is no more than what is naturally expected. The suffering mother does so not out of devotion to her child but because it makes her admirable in the eyes of others. Such hypocrisy encourages women to cleave to victim status and retain power over the child through a guilt that is unwarranted and unviable.

The maternal propensity toward proprietary behavior of the child is evidenced by Madame de Mistival's response to Dolmance's rebuke.

> MADAME DE MISTIVAL. Oh merciful heaven! My Eugenie is doomed, 'tis evident. . . . Eugenie, my beloved Eugenie, for the last time heed the supplications of her who gave you your life; these are orders no longer, but prayers; unhappily, it is only too true that you are amidst monsters here; tear yourself from

> this perilous commerce and follow me; I ask it of you on my knees! (*She falls to her knees.*) (355)

Refusing to fully accept all that Dolmance has said, Madame de Mistival passes judgment on Eugenie's fate, yet the fate is not singularly hers for even in her doom she is still *Madame's* Eugenie as signified by the possessive "my." Madame, who sees the clarity of Eugenie's fall, likens herself to a god empowered by the hubris with which mothers foretell and insist upon (and in this insistence express a desire for) the downfall of their children. She rests her pleas upon the characterization of herself as the one who gave Eugenie her life (yet the use of "her" or more specifically "your" when addressed to Eugenie is not an accurate choice of words and betrays again that paradoxical maternal attitude that refuses to view the child as entirely his or her own person, it is an equation from which the maternal cannot extricate itself without some allusion to its own role in the creation of the child, a role that insists upon calling attention to itself as the child's origin and, therefore, always in possession rather than possessing), insinuating that life remains a gift from mother to child that ought to guarantee the latter's acquiescence.

Unfortunately for Madame de Mistival, who has appealed to Eugenie as one who is at the latter's mercy and whose words may or may not be heeded, Eugenie has been freed to choose for her own self.

> EUGENIE, *half-naked, as the reader surely must remember.* Here you are, my dear little Mamma, I bring you my buttocks. . . . There they are, positively at the level of your lips; kiss them, my sweet, suck them, 'tis all Eugenie can do for you. . . . Remember, Dolmance: I shall always show myself worthy of having been your pupil. (355-56)

By referring to herself in the third person, Eugenie essentially splits herself between what Eugenie as daughter can give her mother and what Eugenie as pupil chooses to give her teacher. In her response is a farewell to herself as child of Madame de Mistival and a willing transference of allegiance to Dolmance. The care that has been "lavished upon" (355) Eugenie and the education which Madame de Mistival credits herself with having provided for her daughter are similarly countered by Dolmance for he explains the need for Eugenie's re-education which "obliged the libertines to replace all the principles [Madame de Mistival] had put into [Eugenie's] head" because "none provide[d] for her happiness" (355).

The invocation of life as gift given from mother to child is met with a sadeian counterpart: life is not a gift but an infliction (Carter, 135), a punishment levied upon the child without so much as a thought. Such a contention refuses any claim of indebtedness on the part of the child to its mother. The randomness and lack of thought that accompany conception, the birthing itself of the child, is in actuality a punishment and to characterize it as anything but that will not be condoned in this world. The gift of life is, therefore, met with its "equal": the punishment of the mother, for inasmuch as she glories in what she has brought forth so must she accept the consequences.

Outraged by Eugenie's behavior, Madame de Mistival again exercises her proprietary rights to Eugenie; this time, however, it is not to re-claim but to abandon her: MADAME DE MISTIVAL, *thrusting Eugenie away, with horror.* "Monster! I disown you forever, you are no longer my child!" Ironically Dolmance demands her punishment for having insulted and "too harshly repulsed" (356) Eugenie. Thus, the mere manner in which she gives up her daughter, severs ties to, decries the child a monster, is the reason cited by Dolmance as necessitating retribution. Implicit in the revocation of her relation to Eugenie is also its assertion proving that even the mother cannot fully extricate herself from the possessive quality that she, herself, has used to define their relationship. Even the verbal characterization of Eugenie as a monster will not be sufficient to create the distance which in Madame de Mistival's mind will make Eugenie other, thus guaranteeing their separation. In this world, Madame de Mistival does not pass judgment but is judged, and the very words with which she condemns Eugenie will come to characterize the manner in which she will be treated as well as the condition to which she will eventually be rendered. This desire to abandon her familial relationship to Eugenie will come to taunt her for in attempting to remove herself from the role of mother, she elicits from Dolmance and Eugenie constant references to her as such, thus proving that it is not always easy to give away that which has always been "yours."

Stuffing

There is in Eugenie a confidence in her manner of speaking to Madame de Mistival that is utterly lacking in Norman and Pentheus. Unlike the stutterings that characterize Norman's speech and the pleas of desperation voiced by Pentheus, confidence and a dry wit mark Eugenie's words: DOLMANCE. "Would you like me to have whips brought in to punish this intractable child?" EUGENIE. "I should be greatly afraid, were they to be sent for, that they would be employed rather upon Madame than upon me" (353). Her statement is a sophisticated one functioning as insult to mother while expressing her own desire for her mother's abuse. In a place where the fulfillment of every desire is pursued, her words serve as an initial sentencing of what her mother is to endure. She is no Norman whose intense struggle with Mrs. Bates is continually played out in a voice that is his own yet dominated by her will, nor is she Pentheus who places himself at the mercy of his mother's "blindness" hoping for an innate recognition of their relationship. Eugenie, first introduced as a girl whose father has to prevent her mother from stopping her departure and who, therefore, must rush to Madame de Saint-Ange becomes a girl who will literally kick her mother in the ass . . . but only after having violated and tortured her first.

> EUGENIE. Come, dear lovely Mamma, come, let me serve you as a husband. . . . Ah, Mother dear, you cry, you scream, scream when your daughter fucks you! . . . Here I am: at one stroke incestuous, adulteress, sodomite, and all that in a girl who only lost her maidenhead today! . . . What progress, my friends! . . . with what rapidity I advance along the thorny road of vice! . . . Oh, right enough, I am a doomed girl! . . . I believe, dear Mother, you are discharging. . . . Dolmance, look at her eyes! She comes, it's certain, is it not? Ah, whore! I'm going to teach you to be a libertine . . . well, bitch, what do you think of that? (*She squeezes, twists, wrenches her mother's breasts.*) Ah, fuck, Dolmance . . . fuck, my gentle friend, I am dying! . . . (*As she discharges, Eugenie showers ten or twelve jarring blows upon her mother's breast and sides.*) (359)

The doom which Madame de Mistival earlier envisions for Eugenie is emphatically and willfully fulfilled upon the (sacred) body of the mother. Given the brutality of the situation in its entirety, it seems overly excessive for Eugenie to punctuate the sexual violation of her mother with the site-specific wringing and punching of her mother's breasts, but in doing so she attacks properties which are crucial to the gestation, eventual birth, and nourishment of an infant. Madame de Mistival's orgasm, however, seems to be have some causal connection to this abuse revealing what may be a masochistic propensity.[7]

If pain, however, is the path to pleasure it would then be possible to read Eugenie's violation of her mother, Madame de Mistival, as an act not simply wrought by pure hatred, but also as a desire to please. If Eugenie has learned from Dolmance as much as she claims and seems to have, then it is impossible for her to ignore that great pain leads to even greater pleasure. Her acts of hatred cannot completely mitigate an irrepressible affection. Eugenie's claim, "I am going to teach you to be a libertine" is not only a wish to become master over her mother but also a desire to share what she has now become with her mother. It is a desire to induct her mother into a lifestyle that Eugenie feels is superior to the one in which the former already takes part. Eugenie annihilates the maternal for the sake of Madame de Mistival's re-birth into a life bereft of the maternal, to elevate her to the status of woman before the contamination of motherhood, and this she accomplishes when the mother orgasms at the hands of her daughter—mother becomes woman at the hands of her daughter. In this scenario, even the mother has to be saved from the maternal, has to be forced to abandon it. As Carter notes, however, Madame de Mistival takes refuge from Eugenie and her inflictions by fainting (128). Unlike the oblivion from which Eugenie emerges as an eager protégé, Madame de Mistival re-gains consciousness only to refuse the lessons being given to her by her daughter. The "life's horrors" into which she is re-awakened testify to her inability to regard herself above the status of victim, a status which had been assigned to her by her abusive husband.

Mutilation/Dismemberment

Unwilling to acknowledge that she too can gain (sexual) pleasure from such brutality, Madame de Mistival proves herself unworthy of the lessons being given. Not only does she embrace her status as victim, but she also refuses to relinquish her status as mother since her last words to her daughter are, "You are tearing me to pieces vile creature! . . . Oh, how I blush that it was I who gave you life!" (364). The act of sewing, not only relegates her to the role of diseased and excrement filled vessel, but it also prevents her from producing/expelling anything, she is not even granted the ability to expel feces. Laying claim to the maternal necessitates the ability to give life, yet Madame de Mistival is a sealed container no longer able to procreate. To return to her womb is to visit death upon the father and the seed.

The wish to possess, which compels maternal vision and is re-translated into the desire to dismember in its failing (as is starkly realized in the actions of Agave), is countered by Eugenie's shocking behavior. Her efforts to resist re-possession by her mother culminate in actions that not only violate but mutilate the maternal body. This is the revelatory moment that coincides with Agave's own: a child's instinct or natural defense mechanism is actually to mutilate its source of origin in an effort to engender itself[8] and break free from that status of possession, object, thing, that owes or is in debt to another.

The wish to dismember counters the biological function of the maternal body, which is to provide a space within which the cells may come together and develop into the fetus. The womb preserves and nurtures, becomes the very space in which the fetus is formed. Yet, conception itself is inspired by fragmentation since the fetal body is formed by the division of cells. For a mother to dismember the living child is paradoxically both an abortive gesture as well as a re-enactment of the child's coming into being. It is a return to a time when the fetus was most an object to be possessed, that is, without its own identity, a thing to be invested with its mother's own perception of it as that to which she has sole ownership. Madame de Mistival's denial of Eugenie as a separate entity, one who is not bound to her mother despite the latter's repeated use of possessive adjectives, is in itself a fragmenting of Eugenie's sense and assertion of self.

To mutilate, however, is the literalization of the impetus to inscribe upon the body. To mutilate or disfigure is an altering of a whole entity into one that lacks completeness. In the case of Madame de Mistival, her failure to return with Eugenie is perversely reflected in the barrenness of her syphilitic womb. Madame de Mistival, who bears the scars of her husband's whip, is depilated, lacerated on her thighs, whipped, embuggered, and anally sewn by Dolmance. Eugenie, who rapes her with a phallus and beats her about the breasts and sides, is said to be "from time to time pricking the lips of the cunt, occasionally stabbing its interior and sometimes using her needle on her mother's belly and mons veneris" for the sake of "simply testing the point" (364), and eventually accomplishes her task of sewing shut her mother's genitalia. Although the anal and vaginal penetrations are indeed punishing it is essential to note the prevalence of markings which Madame comes to bear upon her body. The sealing of the site through which Eugenie first entered the world is a direct assault upon the maternal body and its sanctity.[9] In so mutilating it, the connection between mother and child is not only flouted but reconstituted as a separation between *other* and child. The mutilation has a distancing function that prevents the child from seeing herself reflected in the mother for her body has been retranslated, via the very markings wrought by abuse, into an abhorred thing. In destroying the mother as mirror, the child is allowed the freedom to perceive her own self rather than remaining a passive object to be defined by its origin. Eugenie's definition of self as libertine is achieved through the degradation of her mother as reflection, pursued until it is no longer possible for the image to physically match Eugenie's own. The maternal body whose capacity it is to nurture and comfort cannot be found in the mutilated and, therefore, repugnant body; one does not run to it, rather, one flees.

Madame de Mistival's refusal to believe that Eugenie wishes to remain with the libertines elicits a violent response. Eugenie reverts to a mutilatory act; the truth of her desire becomes literally inescapable once she physically inscribes it upon the denying body. The very truth and declaration of Eugenie's answer is the lived-through tortuous experience that Madame undergoes. In refusing to acknowledge Eugenie's words the first time, Madame is made to live through their writing, thus transforming her into the very testimony/evidence of her own child's disdain. In the case of Eugenie, it is not a desire for a return to the womb[10] that compels her, it is instead a desire to annihilate it. In doing so, Eugenie, herself, begets a thing mutilated—a degraded, sickened, and contaminated vessel that can only breed more disease and death.

The narcissistic aspect that allows the mother to use herself as a veritable dictionary of meaning to ascribe to her child's words is perversely turned upon her, for in mutilating the maternal body, the child forces her to look to herself for its own true meaning. She becomes the site of the child's very own repulsion toward and renouncement of the maternal from which she, herself, cannot escape, the site of a spectacle for her very own eyes. Her gaze is made to be drawn to herself as a site of degradation so much so that the only way in which to avert this vision is to physically faint.

The Sadeian Spectacle and Expulsion

Wrought by the willful and active denial of Eugenie's wish to remain with the libertines, Madame de Mistival is annihilated as maternal subject, that from which she derives her authority over Eugenie. This annihilation, however, is achieved in an orgiastic frenzy that masks the complexity of the event. Along with the command to undress commences the stripping away of Madame de

Mistival as mother, for such trappings only mask her true status as victim. Passive by virtue, morality, and sanctified motherhood,[11] her very body reflects the extremity of her submission and so dictates the manner in which she is to be treated.

> MADAME DE SAINT-ANGE. One moment, gentlemen. Before exposing this charming beauty's body to your gaze, it would be well for me to forewarn you of the condition you are going to find it in. Eugenie has just whispered the entire story into my ear: yesterday, her husband used the whip on her, all but broke his arm, beating her for some minor domestic mismanagement . . . and, Eugenie assures me, you are going to find her ass' cheeks looking more like moiré taffeta.
> DOLMANCE, *immediately Madame de Mistival is naked.* Well, by God, 'tis the absolute truth! I don't believe I've ever seen a body more mistreated than this . . . but, by Jesus! She's got as many cuts before as she has behind! . . . I believe I espy a very fine ass here. (*He kisses and fondles it.*) (356-57)

Here the gaze of the libertines operates under the rubric of revelation and discovery. That which is not ordinarily apparent to the human eye will be rendered so by their gaze. The gaze of the maternal that fixates upon the child as a reflection of itself, that is compelled by a desire to re-possess the child, that will dismember the child in the event of a visual failing, is blindsided by the gaze of the libertine. In its narcissistic fixation the maternal is unprepared for the gaze that does not recognize familial relationships; it is vision with which physical penetration goes hand in hand—a penetration that achieves pleasure for the victimizer and the revelation of truth through pain for the victim. Her prior treatment does not evoke sympathy but instead sanctions their own abuse of her for the very marks coupled with her arrival signify a refusal to accept truth. What Dolmance espies, what he can only glimpse beneath the cuts, will be uncovered, known, and experienced through a physical probing, for in a sadeian world interiority does not function as a boundary one may not cross. Instead, its nature as enclosure beckons its own exposure.

In this particular sadeian world,[12] however, that altering is not expressed in terms of an amputation but in terms of stuffing and of sealing together, creating an illusion of wholeness to the eye, an idea that seems to have intrigued de Sade. De Sade's desire for wholeness seems to first manifest itself in his own personal pursuits of pleasure. Known to travel with a valet, de Sade would pay prostitutes to satisfy his fetishistic desires, but the manner in which he conducted himself and others while engaging in these enjoyments is fascinating. There was a need in de Sade to never lose control while in the throes of pleasure, thus establishing a degree of self-control and self-possession. Instinctual and impulsive behavior, the failure to remember who and what one is, evidenced animalism and a lack of consciousness. Avoidance of this ensures a full appreciation of every act that one commits, done in full knowledge and self-discovery. The baseness of the animal resides in its incapacity to understand itself, to live at the whim of instinct without forethought and reason. To behave in such an unthinking manner contradicts one's existence as a reasoning being. This man, whose characters seem to be so indiscriminately violent and wretchedly impulsive, was governed by a deep need for control and self-discipline. The most private acts become opportunities for spectacles in which he not only imagines the sight of his own behavior, but also physically situates himself as his own watcher. The valet is de Sade not only in the manner of behavior but also in the calling of his name: de Sade. It is this act which allows de Sade to perpetuate the illusion that he is indeed watching himself. The reflection is named and it is that which identifies.

The desire for knowledge of the self is an obsession for de Sade since he is all too aware of the limits of the body. One's self is constantly defined by one's sensory perceptions. It is in this manner that one relates to the world and comes to a deeper understanding of oneself by interpreting the manner in which the world relates to him or her. But this understanding is confined and, more frighteningly, dependent on the participation of an other. Without the other there is no sense of self, but with the other there is also the danger of a misinterpretation of the self. It is this dependence which points to an inability and inherent blind spot within the subjective identity, and it is this which de Sade is aware of. The subject trapped within the body cannot truly see and know itself completely, indicating a lack within one's self-definition. De Sade in his constant efforts to see himself seeing himself implicates this lack, and the frustration with knowing that this lack cannot be made whole manifests itself not only in the disturbing fetishes of his characters, but also in the extreme degree of violence they inflict upon the body.

It is not a mere case of voyeurism which drives de Sade to order his valet to fornicate with a prostitute as he watches, but a desire to observe his own self which becomes apparent in his demand that the valet be acknowledged as the Marquis de Sade, himself. From all sides, de Sade must be able to experience who he is and the manner in which he is perceived. Engaging in such activities is not merely for the sake of enjoyment with the prostitute, but more importantly to exert control over his own behavior, behavior bereft of impulse and instinct which would typically have betrayed him as animalistic human is the means by which he transcends his "humanity." To deny his own identity he must confer it upon another.

At first a participant, he now becomes a spectator, one enabled to watch and experience how another would view him, how another would constitute him as defined by his own behavior. It is one thing for de Sade to be aware of how he defines his own subjectivity; it is another to be able to step outside of the trappings of his own body, which in itself defines his identity, and occupy the place of the gaze, the gaze which sees without feeling and objectifies. Once de Sade occupies this position he becomes the third party, a third witness to his own activities, one whose opinions of himself are shaped by the sight of the valet acting as de Sade.

This concern is reflected in Eugenie's response to the anal stimulation she receives from Dolmance: EUGENIE. "Nothing in the world is so delightful, I do feel that. . . . I am beside myself . . . I no longer know what I am saying, nor what I am doing" (205).[13] Such a claim is reminiscent in sentiment of Pentheus' own when made to see clearly the true face of the god:

> I seem to see two suns blazing in the heavens.
> And now two Thebes, two cities, and each
> with seven gates. And you—you are a bull
> who walks before me there. Horns have sprouted
> from your head. Have you always been a beast?
> But now I see a bull. (ll.918-22)[14]

Eugenie's ecstasy is wrought by physical sensation as opposed to spiritual awareness, thus juxtaposing once again this sadeian prioritizing and supremacy of the body over mind. For Eugenie enlightenment is achieved through sexual demonstrations that awaken the physical senses. Pentheus' body is not without relevance either but it is used in payment for an offense against a god; more importantly, in its dismembered state it is a trophy testifying to his mother's hunting prowess. For these to be accomplished he must be absented from himself, alienated from his own perception as well as his mother's. In this splitting of self that Dionysus orchestrates, Pentheus comes to lack cohesion, which is reflected in his mother's response; she sees no more than a young lion cub, a metaphorical transposition of his utilitarian value as prince and trophy. Eugenie's body is already being put to offensive use, but in pursuit of achieving a heightened sense of self-awareness that secures her identity as a libertine.

There appears to be a difference between the spectacle as discussed in earlier chapters and that which is sadeian despite the fact that each results in the expulsion of a character. In these works, a spectacle is orchestrated, yet there is a difference in the treatment Madame de Mistival receives that goes beyond characterizations such as cruel or vicious. In considering the etymology of spectacle (from the Latin "spectaculum" and "spectare" which mean to look at, to watch, to behold), there is an ingrained object status conferred on that upon which another looks. In these works, however, the characters are not only the center of the spectacle but have invited, even compelled, the gaze of others to fall upon them. Christabel does so by her serpentine behavior wrought by an attempt to reveal the truth about Geraldine to her father. Although Geraldine, herself, exhibits similar behavior it is to a lesser and more subtle degree and resides in the silent exchange of a glance. Norman wears his mother's dress and dons a wig, revealing the identity of "Mother" not only to Sam, Lila, and the audience but to Mrs. Bates, herself, in whose ocular emptiness there can be no reflection of Norman and thus no sense of self. Agave returns with Pentheus' head for the express purpose of self-aggrandizement, pursuing praise and admiration from her family and the citizens of Thebes. These characters remain the focal point but do so from a distance, that is, the spectators do not physically converge upon them. In the case of Madame de Mistival, that distance between her and her libertine audience not only collapses but becomes physically penetrative. Her body becomes the very site upon which the orgiastic spectacle takes place, the object of a gaze imbued with physical power. By virtue of the passivity that attends the sanctification of motherhood, by her unwelcome arrival at the home of Madame Saint-Ange, by her demands for Eugenie's return, Madame de Mistival is literally placed at the very center of the orgiastic spectacle for which Dolmance has such a predilection.

> DOLMANCE. First, Mesdames, you, Saint Ange, and you, Eugenie, have the goodness to arm yourselves with artificial pricks in order, one after the other, to deal this respectable lady, now in the cunt, now in the ass . . . the most fearsome strokes. The Chevalier, Augustin, and I, acting with our own members, will relieve you with prompt exactitude. I am going to begin and, as you may well believe, it is once again her ass which will receive my homage. . . . Augustin, dear boy, console me, by buggering me, for the obligation I am under to sodomize this ancient cow. Eugenie, let me kiss your beautiful behind while I bugger mamma and you, Madame, bring yours near, so that I can handle it . . . socratize it. *One must be walled round by asses when an ass one fucks.* (358) (emphasis mine)

Although Dolmance is obviously the master of ceremonies, Madame de Mistival provides the occasion. Walled around by asses, the mother's is the one to which a perverse "homage" is paid which here is not its worship but its despoiling. Eventually, each member of the group then takes a turn at raping and beating her; she thus becomes an activity in which all can share and partake. In fainting, Madame de Mistival not only demonstrates the extremity of the assault but also an attempt to extricate herself from the situation. This loss of consciousness is a temporary escape from the body around which all have gathered, as well as a "den[ial of] responsibility for her own responses" (Carter, 128). To orgasm from such brutal treatment is a reality that conflicts with the illusion of the mother as moral and non-sexual. This self-denial via fainting prevents this very realization and marks her as a perfect sadeian victim who invites and deserves more abuse: DOLMANCE. "[L]eave her in her swoon. . . . Eugenie, come, stretch out upon your victim's body . . . Chevalier, fuck her as she lies upon her failing mother, and let her frig us, Augustin and me, with each of her hands. You, Saint-Ange, frig her while she's being fucked" (359-360). It is at this point that Madame de Mistival is most objectified for in remaining unconscious she is absent from herself and as such will be brought back to her physical senses, if not her intellectual, in true sadeian fashion: by flogging. The relegation of Madame de Mistival's autonomous body into one of passive location occurs in Eugenie's act of laying upon her mother. In doing so, Eugenie transforms her mother into a literal foundation for their libertine activities. If Madame de Mistival is to refuse intellectual enlightenment and self-awareness then she is taking refuge in the ideologies that the libertines abhor and react against. In physically situating her in this manner, she and that which she represents (virtue, morality, religion, hypocrisy) become implicated in the rise of the libertines, responsible for the very attitudes which they have come to develop. Madame de Mistival as the focal point of their activities is further evidenced by the very manner in which she is later made to kneel in the center while they pass judgment upon her.

The compulsion to look that compels the gaze of others is at the heart of the spectacle, for it is not only the unusual or remarkable that draws our attention. Another word associated with "spectacle" is "gazingstock" or "a person or thing gazed at with scorn or abhorrence; an object of curiosity or contempt."[15] This aspect of abhorrence and contempt runs through and is present in all of these works. It is this which absorbs the gaze to the extent that the expulsion of these characters becomes necessary if we ourselves as readers, and the audience as well as the characters within, are to regain control of their own capacity to gaze. The sadeian spectacle of *Philosophy in the Bedroom* seems to necessitate the expulsion of Madame de Mistival, now rendered unclean and a mere by-product of their libertine pursuits. Such physical degradation differentiates this spectacle from those which occur in the previous texts.

Commanding the gaze of others seems to come at the price of invisibility. Once the focal point, that same character is made to disappear within the confines of the text. In sadeian terms this expulsion of character bears excremental undertones that would corporealize the text itself. Although the child may be subject to the maternal body, the maternal body may at times be vulnerable within the written text. Given the linguistic defense mechanism upon which the sons and daughters in these four works rely, this particular possibility of maternal vulnerability allows the child to circumvent the fragility of the spoken word, the likes of which were useless to Norman, Christabel, and Pentheus.

The Excremental Attitude: Children, Corpses, and Shit

The orifice is of course an aspect of the body which in a sadeian world demands its own degradation. For a man who despises the body for its seemingly bounded and complete appearance (an appearance that can never be entirely seen), the existence of the orifice must be insulting. The body so confident in its wholeness finds this orifice/corporeal space inconsequential in the sense that its nature as a space seems invulnerable and impenetrable, as if its very absence precludes its attack. De Sade confronts the orifice by forcing it to endure fullness, probing it with body parts, stuffing it with excrement, and in Eugenie's sealing it with needle and thread. It is as if de Sade sought to create a new being, someone who by virtue of being physically whole, complete, and orifice-free can only suffer. It is a new creature sent out into the world, its creator identified by the mark of uncompromising wholeness.

By overlaying the psychological affliction of lack upon the body, that absence of and from self, which is hidden in a reflection of wholeness, de Sade illustrates what is absent in strictly corporeal terms. The body is punished for its deceit, as if it had been perpetuating a lie, as if it had claimed that its completeness is a faithful reflection of the psychological state to which it is attached. The self has been defrauded and for that the body must be punished. The actions of de Sade's characters, however, betray a vacillation, the desire to reveal what is incomplete and the inability to fully accept it. De Sade seems to antithetically punish the body, by ripping away skin and filling orifices. He reveals that which was meant to be hidden and fills that which should be empty, thus forcing unnatural conditions upon the body. The eating of excrement in which his characters often indulge themselves is a curiously symbolic act. It bespeaks an effort to assert the body as a completely self-reliant entity, as the center of its own needs with the capacity to satisfy them, thus rendering it self-inclusive.

And yet de Sade's characters reveal an unresolved conflict within the writer, himself, which is the necessary reliance upon others for one's own satisfaction. As in *120 Days of Sodom*, there are characters who do not eat their own excrement, but eat that which is produced by other bodies; this in turn implies a cannibalistic desire on their parts. If consumption is a means of knowing the other, then these characters desire to do just that and not necessarily seek knowledge of themselves. It is as if they feed on the bodies of others in an effort to satisfy their emotional, sexual, and physical appetites—each person exists for another's consumption and that in itself only asserts the dependency upon others which de Sade seems to rebel against. This predilection for coprophilia, the waste products of the body, is a fascination with the body that must, as a biological function, expel and retain a space within itself. The eating of excrement becomes a denial that the body can ever be too full for it eliminates the very evidence of such a process. It denies an emptiness in the bowels, a space in the stomach, a lack within the body. To consume it is to deny that the body has "lost" anything, yet the very act testifies to the need for knowledge of the other if one is to be filled.

Although coprophilia is not a featured practice in *Philosophy in the Bedroom*, it is mentioned as the predilection of Madame de Saint-Ange's husband: MADAME DE SAINT-ANGE. "My husband's whim is to have himself sucked, and here is the most unusual practice joined as a corollary to that one: while, as I bend over him, my buttocks squarely over his face and cheerily pumping the fuck from his balls, I must shit in his mouth! . . . He swallows it down!" (227). Explained by Dolmance as a fashionable addiction for men of a particular age, the manner in which Madame de Saint-Ange describes their occupied position reflects the circularity of this consumptive act. This particular "69" is not the means to an end but an end in and of itself, rather than an act of stimulation that would lead to sexual penetration, it is a singular event that provides for its own culmination. It carries with it an abortive quality, fleeting, nihilistic, cyclical, self-consumed, and consuming. Each is involved in an act of loss and recuperation. The simultaneity of his ejaculation with her bowel movement is a juxtaposition of a life-giving element with waste material. And yet they achieve an equivalence with one another through the very circularity of their exchange.

The multi-faceted role of excrement is also emphasized by the manner in which Dolmance claims anal intercourse ought to be conducted: DOLMANCE. "Full, by all means; 'tis essential the object in use have the most imperious desire to shit, so that the end of the fucker's prick, reaching the turd, may drive deep into it, and may more warmly and more softly deposit there the fuck which irritates and sets it afire" (232). The anal orifice takes on connotations of an anti-womb with its abundance of excrement receiving the ejaculate.

It is in a sense the desire for an excessive wholeness or attempt to fill a space whose nature is to be evacuated (the very etymological root of the name "Mistival"[16] marks her as a perfect site in which this idea is to be enacted) that marks the mother's pursuit as perverse in and of itself. That she bears the name of such significance marks her as *already* discarded material which on a linguistic level further compromises her claim to Eugenie as well as her own efficacy—the womb that must necessarily discard belongs to one already discarded in and through the act of having married. This emptiness within the womb that the maternal seeks to deny via the re-acquisition of the child is perversely fulfilled by Eugenie and her libertine mentors, for they are compelled and justified by Nature. In seeking to re-possess Eugenie, Madame de Mistival seeks to figuratively fill that empty space which is to circumvent the dictates of nature itself. The sadeian punishment in its perversity is to grant that wish by "filling" the space not with the return of Eugenie, but with disease/death.

In *Psycho*, this allusion is maintained by the predominant appearance of Mrs. Bates as shadow. Norman, who preserves her body, can maintain its wholeness but not its integrity. Despite his efforts as a taxidermist, Mrs. Bates remains subject to the dictates of bodily decomposition. More a reminder of death rather than life, the body of Mrs. Bates is in a state of arrested bodily decay. This less than "life-like" preservation of Mother demands that she not only reside within the shadows of the house, but also be depicted as a shadow herself. The ocular orifices from which she "watches over" Norman are a reminder of her absence/death yet Norman cannot resist the impulse to fill his mother's space with his own voice. Mother fills that originary space (that of the womb), by re-possessing Norman at the cost of his own demise, turning him into an empty vessel which she, herself, who is in every sense death, can inhabit. In so doing, the corporeal body that is Norman becomes an orifice. Psychically emptied, he is given the appearance of minimal animation in that final scene with movement limited to his head and facial expression. Yet it is the potency of this expression that signifies the absence of Norman and presence of Mother. Mother comes to don the trappings that were once Norman, transforming him into a mask for herself, as Norman once wore her dress and a wig, thus stressing the utilitarian value that resides within the child for the mother.

The confrontation with the corpse of Mrs. Bates is shocking because it functions as a "misrepresentation" of the manner in which she had been previously encountered. The audience witnesses Mrs. Bates murdering Marion and Arbogast, that is, she is "seen" *in action*. Lila's discovery is a disturbing one because the audience is confronted with the possibility and confusion of a living corpse, a corpse that although dead has taken lives. The interchangeability of Norman for his dead mother, that is, the hoodwinking of the audience, compromises the distinction between the living body and the dead one. In that moment of seeing Mrs. Bates' real face, the viewer automatically absolves her of responsibility for the murders, yet the irony is that even in death she can bring death to others.

The limitation of the corpse as no more than a remainder of a once living body seems to be circumvented by Mrs. Bates. For de Sade there is no such escape. The collective connotations that attend corpus and corps, that is the culminating effect of each, do not extend themselves to the corpse. According to Gallop, the corpse represents the limitation of libertine power. Functioning as the waste material of the struggle between master and slave, the libertine revels in his own power to render another victim, but as corpse it is unable to witness its own defeat that is the libertine's victory. Although an assertion of libertine power, it also functions as a reminder of libertine limitation.[17] However responsible the libertine may be for having taken the life, the power exercised in *taking* a life is mocked by its nature as a momentary event, one that passes out of possession. As such, it will not remain within his grasp, thus depicting the futility of the sadeian enterprise, that endeavor to master another at the cost of the latter's life. All that is left is the body that may bear witness to the master's power, but not recognize and affirm it itself.

This futility, on the other hand, is circumvented in *Philosophy in the Bedroom* for Madame de Mistival is not killed but instead rendered a figuration of death. The momentary event of a life passing out of the libertines' grasp is avoided. Madame de Mistival becomes a product of their desire: a living testament to a libertine victory. This is not to say that there is no impulse toward such a definitive end.

> DOLMANCE. Come, let's gather round our victim: let her kneel in the center of the circle and, trembling, hear what will be announced to her. Madame de Saint-Ange, will you please begin.
> MADAME DE SAINT-ANGE. I condemn her to be hanged.
> LE CHEVALIER. Cut into eighty thousand pieces, after the manner of the Chinese.
> AUGUSTIN. As for me, by Gar, I'd let her off with being broken alive.
> EUGENIE. Into my pretty little mamma's body there will be driven wicks garnished with sulphur and I will undertake to set them afire, one by one. (362)

Eugenie's compulsion to penetrate her mother's body is again echoed by the manner in which she wishes her mother to die. Eugenie's particularity for the lighting of sulphur wicks would obviously not only be torturous, but also render Madame even more repugnant due to its peculiar suffocating odor similar to flatulence which itself is a by-product of the functioning bowels. The idea of the body as waste producing reverberates even in the torture desired by Eugenie for her mother.[18]

Despite these unique suggestions, Dolmance opts for "a little knavery":

> DOLMANCE, *coolly*. I have, waiting outside, a valet, and he is furnished with what is perhaps one of the loveliest members to be found in all of Nature; how-

> ever, it distills disease, for 'tis eaten by one of the most impressive cases of syphilis I have yet anywhere encountered; I'll have my man come in: we'll have a coupling: he'll inject his poison into each of the two natural conduits that ornament this dear and amiable lady, with this consequence: that so long as this cruel disease's impressions shall last, the whore will remember not to trouble her daughter when Eugenie has herself fucked. . . . Lapierre, fuck this woman; she is exceptionally healthy; this amusement might cure you: at least there may be some precedent for the miracle's success. (362-63)

The qualification of Madame de Mistival as "exceptionally healthy" emphasizes the degradation and disease that she will come to bear. Madame de Mistival becomes a perverse expression of motherhood, the discarded waste of the once fecund body now incapable of bringing life to fruition. She is instead made pregnant with disease from which an infection will gestate within her womb mirroring the parasitic nature of the fetus. Unlike the fetus that can be expelled, the disease will remain but retain the potential to spread outward from the confines of her own body should she copulate with another. It is both a fruitlessness of life and the promise of death. In an effort to ensure this, Madame de Saint-Ange suggests she be sewn together. MADAME DE SAINT-ANGE. "I believe it is now of the highest importance to provide against the escape of the poison circulating in madame's veins; consequently, Eugenie must very carefully sew your cunt and ass so that the virulent humor, more concentrated, less subject to evaporation and not at all leakage, will more promptly cinder your bones" (363). According to Bataille, "Life, [de Sade] maintained, was the pursuit of pleasure, and the degree of pleasure was in direct ratio to the destruction of life. In other words, life reached its highest intensity in a monstrous denial of its own principle."[19] In the trials of Madame de Mistival, her status as mother offers an opportunity to destroy life by reaching beyond it to its very origin. And in the sewing and sealing of her anus, Madame de Mistival is transformed into a walking vessel of shit.[20]

The Wandering Mother

The notion of such a mother is perhaps an odd one, for wandering connotes an aimlessness and lack of direction. The woman once a home to a child becomes homeless herself.[21] Characterized by Geraldine as a "wandering mother" the spirit of Christabel's mother is compelled to interfere due to a lack or refusal to recognize her boundaries. This is of course complicated by her existence as a spirit and, therefore, intangible nature. Despite this, she is still seen by Geraldine who in doing so banishes her. Agave who leaves the stage for an "unknown" destination (given the audience's capacity to block out the realization that she indeed is every mother's honest instinct) does not bear any mark of her "crime" against her son, Pentheus. As such she leaves Thebes only to enter another land whose inhabitants may remain unaware of her deeds. Mrs. Bates, in expelling

Norman from his own body, gains the eyes through which she is able to look past the confines of the cinema screen at an audience once comfortable in its own invisibility. For Madame de Mistival, however, there is no one to catch unawares for she will be marked by external, as well as internal, manifestations[22] of her sickness. There is a progression among these characters from the invisible to the visible, from the subtle and insidious to the physically monstrous. From the enclosed space of Madame Saint-Ange's home, Madame de Mistival emerges a perverted creature.

The (Futile) Literality of the Figurative

It is easy to characterize de Sade's writing as lacking originality, as a laundry list of perversions, but that same ease should raise suspicion. De Sade does not devalue the body in his texts, rather, he emphasizes its reality as well as our own. The life of the mind and its intellectual pursuits cannot be divorced from the body for corporeality is the vehicle of our existence.

The brutality of afflictions that surround bodies in de Sade's writings evidences a heightened sense of self-awareness. His many attempts at staging spectacles and occupying positions on the perimeter in an effort to see himself seen indicates an intimate knowledge of how visual perception operates. The impossibility of fully experiencing himself objectively, of re-constructing how others arrive at their opinions of him, is reflected in the repetition of his attempts indicating not success but failure. The intensity of his self-consciousness of others is re-translated as a fixation with the physical body in his texts. His inability to satisfactorily access the figurative, to occupy the place of the other in relation to himself, invests his writings with a shocking literality. The sadeian body becomes a metonymy for the desire of self-awareness and self-recognition. The intensity of his psychological turmoil manifests itself in the particularly extreme physical desecration of others. The invasiveness of the manner in which the sadeian victim is treated inflicts pain as a guarantor of a truth[23] that the victim does not recognize or seeks to deny. If de Sade cannot directly access others' perceptions of him, then his fictional characters will bear the burden of self-discovery in a confrontational and inescapable manner: by way of their own bodies. What de Sade's mind cannot achieve or re-create, physical sensation can with undeniable immediacy.

The consequence of such a sadeian endeavor is the irony of sadism which is illusory not in the pain being given but in the relation of power. The infliction of pain upon another may cast the victimizer in the empowering position, yet it is the victim whose response is sought without which there can be no satisfaction. Sadism may target the body but the victim's pain is necessary to the sadist's enjoyment, thus revealing the victim as the one with power. The illusion of sadism may reveal all too much about de Sade's own endeavors. His proclamations of self-mastery are inaccessible within the realm of reality. His denunciation of a reliance upon others is countered with his inability to occupy the place of the other within his spectacles. Within his fictions, his libertines rely upon their victims to testify to their own power.

Victimizing de Sade: The Lacanian Gaze at Work

Poor de Sade. His many endeavors betray a wish to circumvent a Lacanian condition which he, de Sade, may have proven true by the very futility of these same attempts: "I see only from one point, but in my existence I am looked at from all sides."[24] The simplicity with which this statement is made ignores the intense angst and desperation that de Sade consequently falls victim to. Taken together, Lacan is the figurative and de Sade the literalization of the statement, the concept in action.

> The most radical problem of mimicry is to know whether we must attribute it to some formative power of the very organism that shows us its manifestations. For this to be legitimate, we would have to be able to conceive by what circuits this force might find itself in a position of control, not only the very form of the imitated body, but its relation to the environment, from which is [sic] has to be distinguished, or, on the contrary, in which it has to merge. (73)

What Lacan so clinically and neatly states, de Sade messily demonstrates through his many sexual orchestrations and spectacles, a number of which result in his censure and personal humiliation. Did Lacan, himself, realize the import of his ideas? To put into practice an idea that does not take into account the limitations of the body, that demands we be capable of understanding our being seen from all sides, occupying the place of the other, and evaluating the effects of the environment itself is impossible. The actual attempt and the dedication to its success would leave anyone ranting in sadeian fashion, adamantly professing the supremacy of the body, and eventually suffering from corpulence.

What indeed is the logical conclusion to the Lacanian gaze? With what are we left? Having learned that we ourselves can be the objects of the gaze of an actual object, we are then confronted with ourselves as emptiness, nothingness, absence. And yet, are these not similar or related in consequence to the gaze of the maternal? How beneficial is that realization to Norman and Pentheus? If, in reality, it is true that we can be gazed upon by objects, then Mrs. Bates is mother-object in and of herself. Once "Mother," she is now corpse, without eyes but with the capacity to look, to gaze, to objectify. Her obscene presence melds what she was with what she now is.

Perhaps in the contrivance of the spectacle involving the mother is the mother's attempt to hide the truth that she herself is implicitly and inescapably an object in every sense of its depersonalized connotations. She looks without seeing what is there, without recognizing the child who is before her. Her capacity to objectify, on the other hand, only intensifies her status as object. The biological imperative situates the mother as a location, a place in which the child gestates and eventually emerges. In doing so, the maternal body must necessarily be discarded, an object to be left behind. This is the truth that the maternal seeks to hide. It is not the mother who invests the child with meaning but the child who invests the mother with purpose. She is the Lacanian object who does not see, whose relevance is dependent upon another's (her child's) acquiescence to the idea that one can be seen by that which in truth does not.

Notes

1. "I'm A Mother." Words and music by Chrissie Hynde and James Hood. © 1994 EMI Music Publishing Ltd. and Publisher Unknown. All rights for EMI Music Publishing Ltd. in the U.S. and Canada controlled and administered by EMI April Music Inc. All rights reserved. International copyright secured. Used by permission. "I'm A Mother." By James Hood and Chrissie Hynde. All rights o/b/o Warner Chappell Music Ltd. Administered by WB Music Corp. (ASCAP). All rights reserved. Used by permission. Warner Bros. Publications U.S. Inc., Miami, Florida 33014.

2. Marquis de Sade, *Justine, Philosophy in the Bedroom, and Other Writings*, trans. and comp. Richard Seaver and Austryn Wainhouse (New York: Grove Press, 1965).

3. This aspect of darkness with its connotations of naiveté and secrecy is absent from *Philosophy in the Bedroom*. Eugenie's lessons occur during the day evoking the association of knowledge and the dispelling of specious ideas with light.

4. Unlike Eugenie, who is an active participant in the world of the seen, liberated and welcoming the power of sexual dominance, Christabel is also "fucked" but in a figurative and idiomatic manner. Her emergence seems to trigger or invite another meaning of the word "fuck" which is to be betrayed as signified by Leoline's preference for Geraldine over his own daughter. The very verb is of course a Shakespearean sexual pun. One is either fucked or fucking and it is obvious that the latter is the more desirable position in which to be, active and empowered rather than passive. Given this as well as the connotation of victimization and its use in reference to one who is disliked or more likely despised, fucking itself denotes an absence of emotion particularly affection. This is evidenced by Dolmance's advice to "[n]ever listen to your heart, my child; it is the most untrustworthy guide we have received from Nature" (De Sade, *Philosophy in the Bedroom, and Other Writings,* 340).

5. According to Angela Carter, Eugenie's violation of her mother is authorized by her father. This "faceless authority . . . the father who knows all, sees all and permits almost everything" thus limits the extent to which Eugenie has been freed to act. *The Sadeian Woman* (New York: Pantheon Books, 1978), 131.

6. The maternal gaze informed by the desire to have the child remain within view seems to be at its most urgent, and perhaps most covert, when the father is absent. Madame de Mistival complies albeit through force with Eugenie's departure but then sets out to retrieve her. It seems that in the physical absence of the father and his authority, the mother becomes emboldened and her proprietary feeling toward her child is spurred into action. She, thus, becomes active when father himself is invisible either through a lack of involvement or death. This holds true for Pentheus and Norman whose fathers are

both deceased, and Christabel for whom Leoline has been ineffectual. Monsieur de Mistival may not be present in body, but remains so in word, that is, by way of his letter.

7. For Kristeva, "feminine perversion is coiled up in the desire for law as desire for reproduction and continuity, it promotes feminine masochism to the rank of structure stabilizer (against its deviations); by assuring the mother that she may thus enter into an order that is above that of human will it gives her her reward of pleasure." The self-sacrifice of anonymity "in pass[ing] on the social norm" (*The Kristeva Reader*, 183) can contribute to a jouissance that may very well express itself in the extent to which mothers demand recognition and honor from their children. That Madame de Mistival does achieve a degree of sexual gratification establishes her as a sexual being, a status often denied to and by the figure of the mother. Her response to such brutality testifies to a masochistic propensity rooted in the immediacy of the body, thus, questioning the satisfaction to be found in the psychological reward of pleasure for which she must wait.

8. Eugenie's engendering is discussed by Carter and in Jane Gallop's "The Immoral Teachers," *Yale French Studies* 63 (1982).

9. For Carter, Eugenie's act of sewing is in an effort to free herself by "annihilat[ing] her mother's sexuality" which seems to threaten her own: "The mother wishes Eugenie to behave as if her sexual organs were sealed and therefore Eugenie seals up her mother, to remove the possibility of rivalry, the only reason her mother might possibly have to wish to repress her daughter's sexuality" (117).

10. Returning to the womb is a compulsion toward self-annihilation; mutilation is, thus, an attempt to render the womb undesirable. Achieving realization, that is through one's birth, through a physical existence in the outside world, shuts the door on the possibility of a safe return. Existing within the womb demands a denial of the self as a separate and independent entity from the mother. That maternal power that found expression in the nurturance of the child within the womb can now only be recuperated in its opposite. Having given life, the only way to re-establish that power is to take that same life away. The child that was son or daughter is no longer seen as such but takes on the status of object or animal, something inhuman, that for whom recognition is not obligated. In this case, the fallibility of the eye, its susceptibility to deception, is the means by which vision becomes the conspirator of death, an accomplice in the re-establishment of maternal power.

One who seeks a return to the womb, to the place of one's origins, seeks more than death—(s)he expresses a desire for self-erasure. Death testifies to the existence of a person in the physical world, it is the testimony to a life. Returning to the womb, however, is to come face-to-face with existence lacking merit and consequence—it is the pathway to the realm of the invisible. The fetus is visible only insomuch as it can find expression through an other, the mother's stomach. It is this which saves its physical invisibility from absence. Similarly, the presence of Mrs. Bates is realized by Lila not by the sight of the corpse, but by its impression in the bed, the seemingly exaggerated depth of which expresses a compulsion to sink downward (that being appropriate for the dead) and her association with darker recesses. Ironically Lila interprets this as the sign of a living mother. The fetus, on the other hand, expresses a compulsion to burst forward and out into the world, the proper place for the living. To seek a return to the womb is to, therefore, disturb the natural order and bring about chaos (which would then also suggest that the re-establishment of maternal power signifies disorder).

On a personal note, when my mother feels a heightened affection for me she tells me that she "wishes [she] could put me back in [her] stomach." There is a selfishness there as well as of course the yearning to be united with me once again. It points to a distance which she is incapable of negotiating. But to desire my return to her womb is to desire my disappearance, it is to regret my existence and dismiss my value as a separate entity for the sake of some nostalgic self-completion. Implied in her statement is the belief in her ownership of me, of my status as an object not belonging to her and my father but to her alone. It points to both a physical and emotional void left by my expulsion.

11. See the chapter entitled, "The Desecration of the Temple" in Carter's *The Sadeian Woman*, 38-77.

12. In de Sade's *120 Days of Sodom*, however, amputations run rampant [Marquis de Sade, *The 120 Days of Sodom and Other Writings*, trans. and comp. Austryn Wainhouse and Richard Seaver (New York: Grove Weidenfeld, 1966)]. As much as de Sade rails against mothers and their knowing the true identities of their children, the violence that he depicts in this text is just as much about children as well. It is as if he cannot extricate one from the other, one contaminating and demanding the other's desecration.

13. The translation by Meredith X. reads: "I am beside myself, I no longer recognize, my own actions." Marquis de Sade, *Philosophy in the Boudoir*, trans. Meredith X., ed. Julian Jones (N.p.: Creation Books, 2000), 30.

14. Euripides, *The Bacchae*, trans. William Arrowsmith, in *Euripides V: Three Tragedies*, ed. David Grene and Richmond Lattimore (Chicago: University of Chicago Press, 1959).

15. Webster's Revised Unabridged Dictionary, © 1996, 1998 MICRA, Inc.

16. According to Gallop, "the English word 'misty' although sharing no etymological relation to 'mystery,' 'mystic' etc . . . carries a similar meaning of 'obscure, clouded' . . . 'mist' stems from an Indo-European root 'meigh' which means 'to urinate,' and which also produces 'micturate' and 'mistletoe'" ("The Immoral Teachers," 124).This seems to point to an inherent wastefulness in the figure of the mother, perhaps in the pointlessness of her role as nurturer which of course de Sade doesn't feel should be her role, but also indicates a necessarily disposable quality to the maternal, that which must be discarded.

17. Jane Gallop, *Intersections: A Reading of Sade with Bataille, Blanchot, and Klossowski* (Lincoln: University of Nebraska Press, 1981), 44.

18. Sulphur is also used in the manufacturing of insecticides and calls to mind the matronly woman in the hardware store from *Psycho* who muses, "They tell you what its ingredients are, and how it's guaranteed to exterminate every insect in the world, but they do not tell you whether or not it's painless. And, I say, insect or man, death should always be painless." With this in mind, it is difficult to avoid the depiction of Madame de Mistival as pesky and inconsequential, a characterization that surely fits within the text.

19. Georges Bataille, *Erotism: Death and Sensuality*, trans. Mary Dalwood (San Francisco: City Lights, 1986), 180.

20. Or as was once a common derogatory expression: "[You're] a bag of shit."

21. In the randomness of such movement there also resides that potential for a transgression. Whereas her status as mother purposefully sanctioned such behavior toward her child, this propensity can now only be accessed by chance and upon others over whom she has no right.

22. "During the first stage, the *Primary stage*, painless ulcers called chancres occur on the genitalia, anus, fingers, lips, tongue, tonsils or eyelids. Women may develop chancres on the cervix or vaginal wall. The *Secondary stage* begins within a few days or up to eight weeks after the ulcers appear. Symptoms include headache, nausea, vomiting, fatigue, appetite and weight loss, sore throat and slight fever. A rash can occur on arms, palms, soles, face and scalp. Drainage that occurs from this rash is highly contagious. Some people experience hair loss. In the *Late stage*, symptoms depend on which organs the disease has invaded. If it has invaded the nervous system, headache, dizziness, sleeplessness, seizures and psychosis may develop. Lesions, called gummas, may occur on the

skin, bones or any body organ. These lesions are usually painless but can be disfiguring. Syphilis can also affect the heart and kidneys." University of Missouri-Rolla, www.umr.edu/~umrshs/sexual_health/syphillis.html (15 July 2002).

23. David B. Morris, "The Marquis de Sade and the Discourses of Pain: Literature and Medicine at the Revolution," *The Languages Clark Library Lectures 1985-1986*, ed. G.S. Rousseau (University of California Press, 1990), 291-330. www.usipp.com/rfrancka/download/Sade%20Marquis%20de/Morris%20Essay.doc (15 July 2002).

24. Jacques Lacan, *The Four Fundamental Concepts of Psycho-Analysis*, trans. Alan Sheridan, ed. Jacques-Alain Miller (New York: W.W. Norton & Co., 1977), 72.

Conclusion

Eyeing the Margins

> "She did what she thought was right in her perception of the world through her psychotic eyes."
>
> —forensic psychiatrist Phillip Resnick's testimony at the trial of Andrea Yates, the woman found guilty in the drowning deaths of her five children[1]

Having begun with *The Bacchae* and concluded with *Philosophy in the Bedroom* was not without purpose. The particular texts and movie with which I work may appear to suggest that any struggle between mother and child will in all likelihood result in the mother's victory or ascendancy. It is incorrect to believe that the child will never strike back, that within the child filial affection will allow him to tolerate his subjection to the mother's whim let alone destructive tendencies. That is as much folly as it is to believe that a mother harbors no ill feelings toward her own child. Once engaged in this struggle, only one will be left standing or at least remain within the world of the text. At risk is not only one's literal existence but also a *literary* existence. Expulsion from Thebes, the home of Madame de Saint-Ange, and from the text itself only heralds an arrival in another place, rather than the finality of a disappearance. Agave and Madame de Mistival walk away, but to where? A more marginal space? Yet what constitutes margins can often be larger than the spaces afforded to the written word, for the reader becomes the margin itself in whom these mothers will settle and reside.

What the reader is then confronted with is the look into the mirror that Norman Bates cannot bring himself to endure. If one finds the actions of the mother reprehensible what then is the response? Although Agave has dismembered Pentheus, Mrs. Bates has psychically possessed Norman, and the spirit of Christabel's mother has imprisoned Christabel within a realm void of experience that eventually demands her traumatic encounter with the maternal substitute Geraldine, do any of these match the shock and brutality that Eugenie's sewing of her mother's genitalia elicits? How horrid the child must be who is capable of doing such a thing! Although the mother may see the child as an extension of her own self thereby characterizing him as a fragment, the child does not see himself as such. He knows he is an independent entity, whole unto himself. It is better to wound the mother than kill her for the scar will remain the mark of her failure.

It is easier to rid oneself of her child than it is for the child to rid himself of his mother, but if the latter makes the attempt it does not demand the mother's death as much as it does her mutilation or disfigurement. The mother will kill her child for who he is or fails to be with the right given to one who possesses an object; the child will mutilate the mother to annihilate his own origin, to destroy the very link that binds them together.

Notes

1. "Yates claimed she killed kids to keep them from going to hell," CourtTV.com, www.courttv.com/trials/yates/030102_pm.html (1 March 2002). Reproduced by permission of the Courtroom Television Network LLC.

Selected Bibliography

Achilles Tatius. *Leucippe and Clitophon*. Translated by John J. Winkler. In *Collected Ancient Greek Novels*, edited by B.P. Reardon, 170-284. Berkeley: University of California Press, 1989.

Anobile, Richard J., ed. *Alfred Hitchcock's Psycho*. New York: Universe Books, 1974.

Bataille, Georges. *Erotism: Death and Sensuality*. Translated by Mary Dalwood. San Francisco: City Lights, 1986.

Bellour, Raymond. "Psychosis, Neurosis, Perversion." In *A Hitchcock Reader*, edited by Marshall Deutelbaum and Leland Poague, 311-331. Ames: Iowa State University Press, 1986.

Brill, Lesley. *The Hitchcock Romance: Love and Irony in Hitchcock's Films*. Princeton, NJ: Princeton University Press, 1988.

Bryson, Norman. *Vision and Painting: The Logic of the Gaze*. New Haven, CT: Yale University Press, 1983.

Carter, Angela. *The Sadeian Woman and the Ideology of Pornography*. New York: Pantheon Books, 1978.

Chion, Michel. "The Impossible Embodiment." In *Everything You Always Wanted to Know About Lacan (But Were Afraid to Ask Hitchcock)*, edited by Slavoj Zizek, 195-207. London: Verso, 1992.

Coleridge, Samuel Taylor. "Christabel." In *English Romantic Writers*, 2nd ed., edited by David Perkins, 529-537. New York: Harcourt Brace, 1995.

Cryle, Peter. *Geometry in the Boudoir: Configurations of French Erotic Narrative*. Ithaca, NY: Cornell University Press, 1994.

Desmond Morris' The Human Sexes: Languages of the Sexes. Directed by Dan McCabe and Bob Burns. TLC, 1997.

Euripides. *The Bacchae*. Translated by William Arrowsmith. In *Euripides V: Three Tragedies*, edited by David Grene and Richmond Lattimore, 141-220. Chicago: University of Chicago Press, 1959.

Euripides. *The Bacchae. The Perseus Digital Library.* Edited by T.A. Buckley.

www.perseus.tufts.edu/cgi-bin/ptext?doc=Perseus%3Atext%3A1999.01.0092 (1 July 2001).

Euripides. *The Bacchae*. Translated by Moses Hadas and John McLean. In *Ten Plays by Euripides*. New York: Bantam Books, 1981.

Flory, Wendy Stallard. "Fathers and Daughters: Coleridge and 'Christabel.'" *Women and Literature* 3.1 (Spring 1975): 5-15.

Gallop, Jane. "The Immoral Teachers." *Yale French Studies* 63 (1982): 117-182.

———. *Intersections: A Reading of Sade with Bataille, Blanchot, and Klossowski*. Lincoln: University of Nebraska Press, 1981.

Geyer-Ryan, Helga. "Imaginary Identity: Space, Gender, Nation." In *Vision in Context: Historical and Contemporary Perspectives on Sight*, edited by Teresa Brennan and Martin Jay, 117-125. New York: Routledge, 1996.

Goldhill, Simon. "Refracting Classical Vision: Changing Cultures of Viewing." In *Vision in Context: Historical and Contemporary Perspectives on Sight*, edited by Teresa Brennan and Martin Jay, 15-28. New York: Routledge, 1996.

Graves, Robert. *The Greek Myths*. Mt. Kisco: Moyer Bell Ltd., 1988.

Hoeveler, Diane Long. *Romantic Androgyny: The Women Within*. University Park: Pennsylvania State University Press, 1990.

Kristeva, Julia. *The Kristeva Reader*. Edited by Toril Moi. New York: Columbia University Press, 1986.

———. *Powers of Horror: An Essay on Abjection*. Translated by Leon S. Roudiez. New York: Columbia University Press, 1982.

Lacan, Jacques. *The Four Fundamental Concepts of Psycho-Analysis*. Translated by Alan Sheridan and edited by Jacques-Alain Miller. New York: W.W. Norton & Co., 1977.

Morris, David B. "The Marquis de Sade and the Discourses of Pain: Literature and Medicine at the Revolution." *The Languages Clark Library Lectures 1985-1986*. Edited by G.S. Rousseau. N.p.: University of California Press, 1990. www.usipp.com/rfrancka/download/Sade%20Marquis%20de/Morris%20Essay.doc (15 July 2002).

Mulvey, Laura. *Visual and Other Pleasures*. London: Macmillan, 1989.

Nelson, Jane. "Entelechy and Structure in 'Christabel.'" *Studies in Romanticism* 19 (Fall 1980): 375-393.

Nethercot, A.H. *The Road to Tryermaine; A Study of the History, Background, and Purposes of Coleridge's "Christabel."* Chicago: University of Chicago Press, 1939.

Poague, Leland. "Links in a Chain: *Psycho* and Film Classicism." In *A Hitchcock Reader*, edited by Marshall Deutelbaum and Leland Poague, 340-349. Ames: Iowa State University Press, 1986.

Recchia, Edward. "Through a Shower Curtain Darkly: Reflexivity as a Dramatic Component of *Psycho*." *Literature Film Quarterly* 19.4 (1991): 258-267.

Rothman, William. *Hitchcock the Murderous Gaze*. Cambridge: Harvard University Press, 1982.

Sade, Marquis de. *The 120 Days of Sodom and Other Writings.* Translated by Austryn Wainhouse and Richard Seaver. New York: Grove Weidenfeld, 1966.

———. *Justine, Philosophy in the Bedroom, and Other Writings.* Translated and compiled by Austryn Wainhouse and Richard Seaver. New York: Grove Press, 1965.

———. *Philosophy in the Boudoir*. Translated by Meredith X. and edited by Julian Jones. N.p.: Creation Books, 2000.

Salecl, Renata, and Slavoj Zizek, eds. *Gaze and Voice as Love Objects*. Durham: Duke University Press, 1996.

Segal, Charles. *Dionysiac Poetics and Euripides' Bacchae*. Expanded ed. Princeton: Princeton University Press, 1982.

Silverman, Kaja. "From *The Subject of Semiotics* (On Suture)." In *Film Theory and Criticism*, 5th ed., edited by Leo Braudy and Marshall Cohen, 137-147. New York: Oxford University Press, 1999.

Soskice, Janet. "Sight and Vision in Medieval Christian Thought." In *Vision in Context: Historical and Contemporary Perspectives on Sight*, edited by Teresa Brennan and Martin Jay, 29-43. New York: Routledge, 1996.

Spoto, Donald. *The Dark Side of Genius: The Life of Alfred Hitchcock*. New York: DeCapo Press, 1983.

Stefano, Joseph. *Alfred Hitchcock's Psycho*. Directed by Alfred Hitchcock. 109 min. Universal City: Universal Home Video, 1998. DVD.

Sterritt, David. *The Films of Alfred Hitchcock*. New York: Cambridge University Press, 1993.

Stock, R.D. *The Flutes of Dionysus: Daemonic Enthrallment in Literature*. Lincoln: University of Nebraska Press, 1989.

Spatz, Jonas. "The Mystery of Eros: Sexual Initiation in Coleridge's 'Christabel.'" *PMLA* 90.1 (January 1975): 107-116.

Starobinski, Jean. *The Living Eye*. Translated by Arthur Goldhammer. Cambridge: Harvard University Press, 1989.

Swann, Karen. "Christabel and the Enigma of Form." *Studies in Romanticism* 23 (Winter 1984): 533-553.

Winnicott, D.W. *Psycho-Analytic Explorations*. Edited by Clare Winnicott, Ray Shepherd, and Madeleine Davis. Cambridge: Harvard University Press, 1989.

"Yates claimed she killed kids to keep them from going to hell." CourtTV.com. www.courttv.com/trials/yates/030102_pm.html (1 March 2002).

Index

abortion, 16, 25, 79, 84, 91
Agave, 6-7, 11, 13, 15, 16, 19, 20, 22, 23, 24-27, 29n12, 29n16, 30n21, 30n23, 78, 79, 84, 88, 94

The Bacchae, 4, 5, 6, 10, 12n6, 13-27, 99n14
Bataille, Georges, 94, 99n17, 99n19
Bates, Norma, 74n8, 92-93; corpse of, 57, 63, 66, 67, 72, 73, 90, 92-93, 96, 98n10; gaze of, 53, 55, 57, 65, 72-73, 75n16, 94-95, 96-97
Bates, Norman, 10, 18, 76n17, 77; linguistic failure of, 56, 57, 58-61, 63-65, 66, 68-69, 71, 74n6, 82, 88, 90
blindness, 25, 44, 48, 54, 78, 82

Cadmus, 7, 26, 30n22, 30n23
Carter, Angela, 80-81, 83, 89; *The Sadeian Woman*, 97n5, 98nn8-9, 99n11
child: as object, 4-7, 9-10, 13-14, 16-20, 26, 39, 41-42, 48-50, 55, 72, 81, 82, 84-85, 92, 97, 98n10, 102; as indebted, 14, 21, 79-81, 84
Christabel, 4, 8-10, 12n8, 31-52, 77, 79, 88, 94, 97n4, 97n6; linguistic failure of, 11, 36-37, 44, 46-50, 90
Christianity, 51n10, 79, 89; prayer and, 31, 35-36, 37, 38, 42-44, 48, 80; Virgin Mary, 35, 36, 50n5
Coleridge, Samuel Taylor, 4, 8, 12n8, 31, 50, 50n2, 50n6, 51n9, 51n11, 51nn15-16
conception, 5, 25, 36, 77, 81, 84, 96
coprophilia, 4, 91. *See also* excrement
corpse, 24
Crane, Marion, 64-65; gaze of, 53-54, 72; lingustic failure of, 57-58, 67-68; death of, 66, 69, 70, 75n14, 92

Dionysus, 5, 6, 13, 14-17, 22-23, 26, 27nn2-3, 27n8, 29n14, 30n22, 88
dismemberment, 6, 11, 14, 16, 22, 25, 61, 77, 84-86, 98n10, 102. *See also* Pentheus
Dolmance, 7, 78, 80-81, 82, 83, 84, 86, 87, 89, 91, 93, 97n4

Eugenie de Mistival, 7-8, 77; liberation of, 81-82, 84-85, 88-89, 93-95, 98n9; linguistic success of, 82-83
Euripides, 4, 12n6, 13, 26, 27nn3-4, 27n7, 29n12, 30n21, 99n14
excrement, 8, 84, 90-92

father, 10, 27n8, 37, 49-50, 52n16, 80, 84, 97nn5-6
femininity, 37-38, 44, 47, 49, 50n5, 52n18, 98n7
filicide, 12n4, 26, 29n14, 70

Gallop, Jane, 50n4, 93, 98n8, 99nn16-17
Geraldine, 8-9, 11, 31-52, 77, 88, 94,

97n4; gaze of, 39-40, 44-48, 51n13; as surrogate mother, 38-39, 43

incest, 77, 83
infanticide, 79

Lacan, Jacques, 27, 75n8, 96-97, 100n24
language acquisition, 17-19
Leoline, 9, 32, 33, 34, 36, 37, 38, 39, 40-42, 46-50, 52n18, 97n4, 97n6
libertinage, 7, 77-81, 83, 85-86, 88-90, 92, 96; limitations of, 93

maiden, 31, 36, 38, 40, 43, 45
masculinity, 31, 36-38, 40, 49, 57, 75n16
maternal instinct, 12n4, 14, 19-27, 79, 94
Mistival, Madame de, 7-8, 78-82, 97n6, 98n7, 99n16, 99n21; defilement of, 82-86, 88-89, 93-95
Mistival, Monsieur de, 79, 80, 82, 97n6
morality, 5, 29n14, 38, 50n4, 52n16, 79, 86, 89, 98n8, 99n16
mother: as devouring, 9, 13, 19-21, 73; unconscious hatred toward child, 14, 23, 28n9, 29n15
mother-child bond, 5-6, 7, 17, 29n14, 32, 39, 42, 77, 78, 80; and narcissism, 4, 14, 23-24, 40, 50n5, 85-86
motherhood: condemnation of, 39, 79, 83, 93-94, sanctification of, 8, 24, 86, 89
mummification, 56, 63, 75n9, 75n15. *See also* taxidermy
mutilation. *See* dismemberment

orgy, 77, 85, 88-89

Pentheus, 5, 28n8, 29n15, 77, 78, 96, 97n6; death of, 6-7, 11, 20, 26-27, 29n12, 29n16, 30n18, 30n23, 88, 94; linguistic failure of, 14-17, 19, 21-22, 82, 90; as trophy, 23-25
Philosophy in the Bedroom, 4, 5, 7, 10, 12n7, 77-100
pregnancy, 4-5, 11, 27n8, 28n11, 39-40, 42, 94; gestation period and, 34, 83, 97. *See also* womb
Psycho, 4, 8, 10, 53-76, 92, 99n18

reflection, 3, 4, 6, 16, 24, 25, 27, 47, 54, 56, 67, 70, 74, 75n12; of Marion Crane, 55, 61-62; of Norman Bates, 62, 73

Sade, Marquis de, 4, 6, 11, 12n7, 80-81, 85-87, 90-91, 93, 94, 95, 96-97, 99n12. See also *Philosophy in the Bedroom*
sadism, 77, 79, 88-89, 92
Saint-Ange, Madame de, 77, 78-80, 82, 86, 89, 91, 93, 94, 95
sodomy, 77, 79, 83, 89
sterility, 34, 47, 77
syphilis, 8, 84, 94, 99n22

taxidermy, 10, 71, 72, 75n11, 75n15, 92
touch, 6, 9, 14, 22, 25, 29n12, 34, 39, 46, 47, 60, 72

vision, 14, 19-20, 22, 28n9, 40, 48, 54-55, 64, 72-73, 84-85, 98n10; classical view of, 51n10, 51n14, 52n18; eye and, 1-5, 9-10, 11n1, 12n2, 50n3, 50n8, 74n3
voice, 2, 6, 10, 15-16, 18, 23, 29nn15-16, 38, 47, 53, 56, 59, 63-64, 73, 75n8, 82, 92
voyeurism, 45, 74n2, 87

Winnicott, D.W., 14, 19, 27n6, 28n9, 29nn15-16, 30n19
womb, 4, 5, 98n10; in "Christabel," 8-9, 19, 21, 31, 34-38, 39-40, 41-42, 43, 47-48, 77; in *Philosophy in the Bedroom*, 79, 84-85, 92, 94

Yates, Andrea, 101, 102n1

About the Author

Alina M. Luna received her Ph.D. in English in 2002 and is currently an adjunct instructor at the State University of New York at Albany and Siena College. A first-generation Filipino-American, her fields of interest and expertise include nineteenth-century British literature, Greek myth and drama, cultural studies, and literary perversions. She is currently working on a project on academic daughters.